T0305823

Shaking up Measures of
**Consumer Economic
Well-being**

Shaking up Measures of
Consumer Economic
Well-being

Thijs ten Raa
Utrecht School of Economics, The Netherlands

World Scientific

NEW JERSEY · LONDON · SINGAPORE · BEIJING · SHANGHAI · HONG KONG · TAIPEI · CHENNAI · TOKYO

Published by

World Scientific Publishing Co. Pte. Ltd.

5 Toh Tuck Link, Singapore 596224

USA office: 27 Warren Street, Suite 401-402, Hackensack, NJ 07601

UK office: 57 Shelton Street, Covent Garden, London WC2H 9HE

Library of Congress Cataloging-in-Publication Data

Names: ten Raa, Thijs, author.

Title: Shaking up measures of consumer economic well-being / Thijs ten Raa.

Description: Hackensack, NJ : World Scientific Publishing Co. Pte. Ltd., [2022] |
    Includes bibliographical references and index.

Identifiers: LCCN 2022006959 | ISBN 9789811249785 (hardcover) |
    ISBN 9789811251795 (ebook) | ISBN 9789811251801 (ebook other)

Subjects: LCSH: Consumers--Research. | Consumer behavior.

Classification: LCC HF5415.32 .R323 2022 | DDC 658.8/34--dc23/eng/20220321

LC record available at https://lccn.loc.gov/2022006959

British Library Cataloguing-in-Publication Data

A catalogue record for this book is available from the British Library.

For any available supplementary material, please visit
https://www.worldscientific.com/worldscibooks/10.1142/12656#t=suppl

Desk Editor: Lum Pui Yee

Typeset by Stallion Press
Email: enquiries@stallionpress.com

Printed in Singapore

About the Author

Thijs ten Raa is a lecturer and researcher at the Utrecht School of Economics in The Netherlands. Professor ten Raa's primary research area is economic theory. He has published thirteen books, including the acclaimed textbooks *The Economics of Input-Output Analysis*, Cambridge University Press (2005) and *Microeconomics: Equilibrium & Efficiency*, Palgrave Macmillan (2013), and numerous articles in publications including *Economics Letters*, *Journal of Economic Theory*, *Review of Economics and Statistics*, *International Economic Review*, *Review of Income and Wealth*, *Journal of Productivity Analysis*, *Journal of Banking and Finance*, *Journal of Economic Behavior and Organization* and *Oxford Economic Papers*. In 2006 he shared the Wassily Leontief Centennial Medal with Professors Klein and Solow. In 2013 he was elected fellow of the International Input-Output Association.

Contents

Chapter 1

Introduction

In this book, I analyze measures of consumer well-being. Recently (2020), I wrote a paper in a special issue of the *International Journal of Economic Theory* to honor my colleague and friend Marcus Berliant. I argued that a variant of consumer's surplus, the consumer's index, is a superior measure for demands without income effects. This raises several questions. When and why is a measure superior? What is the extent of the result? Is not consumer's surplus a concept limited to the special, hence uninteresting no-income effects case? Is it extendable at all to cases with income effects? What about aggregate demands? And should not consumer well-being be a broader concept than one based on demand functions? If so, can the consumer's index accommodate non-market indices? Roughly speaking, this monograph provides affirmative, qualified answers to these questions.

The three main, neoclassical measures of well-being are the compensating variation, the equivalent variation, and consumer's surplus. Consumer's surplus is the easiest, it is defined as the difference between the willingness to pay for the different units consumed and the pay, i.e. price. It is measured by the area between the ordinary demand curve and the price line. When a price changes, the variation of consumer's surplus is the area under the ordinary demand curve between the two price lines. The compensating and equivalent variations are similar surplus measures, but with the ordinary demand curve replaced by a so-called compensated demand curve, along which the utility of the consumer is held constant (by side payments), at the initial utility level in case of the compensating variation, and at the new utility level in case of the equivalent variation. All three surplus measures are central economic concepts. As McFadden (2014) states,

> 'Neoclassical measurement of well-being starts from the assumption that one can identify and recover the market demand functions of individuals and infer from these the features of the money-metric utility necessary to do the consumer surplus calculation.'

There is a connection between the surplus measures and the theory of price indices. Prices change all the time, at different rates. How do we summarize these changes in an index? There are statistical and economic approaches to this problem. I focus on the latter but will relate to the former. In fact, the measures of consumer well-being are the core of the economic approach to price indices. The question is, which of the measures of consumer well-being is the best? This book tackles the question, with a surprising outcome, contrary to the main opinion in the literature.

The economic measures of consumer well-being will be defined formally in Chapters 3 and 4 and account for the effect of income changes, but the intuition can be given in the simple case that only price changes. The compensating variation is defined as the amount of money that must be given to the consumer to compensate him for the loss of well-being due to the price changes. This measure, due to Hicks (1942), the inventor of the compensating demand curves, has supreme status among economists. Hausman (1981) states:

'It is my feeling of the situation that substantial agreement exists on the correct quantities to be measured: the amount the consumer would pay or would need to be paid to be just as well off after the price change as he was before the price change. The quantities correspond to John Hicks' compensating variation measures.'

The equivalent variation is the amount of money that could have been taken from the consumer instead of changing the prices. This measure, also due to Hicks (1942), is a close twin of the compensating variation. If the price system changes from vector p to vector p', then the equivalent variation equals the compensating variation associated with the reverse price system change, from p' to p. The compensating variation is forward looking, with the new price system as the basis for the subsidy calculation. The equivalent variation is backward looking, with the old price system as the basis for the tax calculation. Both measures have the status of exact measures. Mishan (1977) comments on the compensating variation and equivalent variations:

'They are both exact measures of the welfare change in question. They are in principle measurable, and — in an allocative context — they define the required valuation.'

Consumer's surplus is the best-known measure. As said, it is based on the difference between the value of commodities a consumer is willing to pay and price. This measure, due to Marshall (1920), is practical, because it can be measured by the area between the demand curve (revealing the willingness to pay) and the price line (the pay). However, among economists the status of consumer's surplus is low. For example, in a widely cited paper Willig (1976) writes:

'I will show that observed consumer's surplus can be rigorously utilized to estimate the unobservable compensating and equivalent variations — the correct theoretical measures of the welfare impact of changes in prices and income on an individual.'

This sounds fine, but Willig sides with the presumption that consumer's surplus is an approximation at best, while Bruce (1977) is more forceful:

'As a case in point, consider the suggestion that consumer's surplus measures be abandoned in favor of the path independent compensating or equivalent variations (Mohring, 1971, p. 362; Silberberg, 1972, pp. 950–951). If such alternatives were operational, that would end the issue, but they are not.'

A further blow to the measure of consumer's surplus has been given by Hausman (1981). He builds on the theory that recovers indirect utility from demand (Samuelson, 1947; Hurwicz and Uzawa, 1971). This theory works for individual demand functions, which are derived by maximizing utility subject to a budget constraint. The derivation involves differentiation. Conversely, from an individual demand function one can recover the indirect utility function by integration. This enables the analyst to derive all measures, not only the demand-based consumer's surplus, but also compensated demand and, thereby, the compensating and equivalent variations. Consumer's surplus is an approximation, but if there are sufficient data, you can estimate the compensating and equivalent variations without using consumer's surplus.

The knockout has been delivered by Deaton (1986, pp. 1828–1829):

'Geometrically, calculating compensating variation or equivalent variation is simply a matter of integrating the area under a *Hicksian* demand curve; there is no valid theoretical or practical reason for ever integrating under a *Marshallian* demand curve. The very considerable literature discussing the practical difficulties of doing so (the path-dependence of the integral, for example) provides a remarkable example of the elaboration of secondary nonsense which can occur once a large primary category error has been accepted; the emperor with no clothes, although quite unaware of his total nakedness, is continuously distressed by his inability to tie his shoelaces.'

The verdict seems clear. In the race of the best well-being measure, the winner is compensating variation, second best is equivalent variation, and the looser is consumer's surplus. However, in a neglected paper Takayama (1982) has shown that the Hicksian compensating and equivalent variations are not the correct measures of consumer well-being, while consumer's surplus, albeit normalized by income, is, at least for homothetic demands (which grow proportionally with income). A short proof of this result has been given recently by ten Raa (2017). The measures are shaken up. What is going on here? The measures integrate changes due to price and possibly income changes. The literature, particularly Silberberg (1972), has stressed that such measures better be path independent. This is how the Hicksian variations defeated the Marshallian surplus. Takayama (1982) basically argued that path independence is not the issue. The issue is that a measure tracks utility. This is the point of departure in my analysis. In fact, it is the organizing principle of the book.

In this chapter, I present a test that measures must pass to track utility. The test will be used to sort measures in the remainder of the book. It will culminate in a variant of consumer's surplus, which I called the consumer's index, and a generalization that applies to nonhomothetic demands. The emperor does not want to tie his shoelaces; the emperor is not totally naked.

What determines the well-being of the consumer? The economist's answer is simple. It depends on the quantities of goods and services consumed. Moreover, the valuation is specific to each consumer. Consumers have different tastes. In this monograph I make a shortcut by summarizing the taste of a consumer in a utility function. List the goods and services, from 1 to n. Denote the quantities consumed by a consumer as $x_1, \ldots, x_n$, respectively, and stack these quantities in vector x, the consumption bundle. The consumer attaches utility $U(x)$ to the consumption bundle. No absolute value is attached. All that is relevant is that utility function U sorts what is preferred by the consumer. If the consumer may choose between alternative consumption bundles, say x and x', and selects x, not x', then $U(x) > U(x')$. All that is relevant is this order of $U(x)$ and $U(x')$, not their levels. Instead of utility function U, we may just as well use $2U$, or even a nonlinear monotonic transformation of U, because it preserves the order. The utility function is ordinal, not cardinal. However, the utility function is consumer specific. Economists consider it to be a given, leaving the explanation of taste to psychologists.

A problem of utility functions is that they are not observed. It is pointless to measure the well-being of a consumer by the utility attained, if only because we could just as well take double the value. A better point of departure is the choice consumers make, the demand they exercise in the market. Let the prices of the goods and services be given by $p_1, \ldots, p_n$, and let the available budget be given by m. All quantities, prices, and the budget are nonnegative numbers. The expenditure is $px = p_1 x_1 + \cdots + p_n x_n$, where p is the price (row) vector. The budget set is the set of all commodity bundles x which are affordable, meaning $px \leq m$. Commodities is the collective term for goods and services. The consumer will select the best available bundle, that is with the greatest utility, by maximizing $U(x)$ subject to the budget constraint, $px \leq m$. The choice remains the same if we replace utility function U by a monotonic transformation, confirming the ordinal nature of utility.

The problem of the consumer is $\max_x U(x) : px \leq m$. The solution to the problem depends on the parameters the consumer faces, that is price vector p and budget m. In other words, the choice of the consumer is a function of price and income: $x = D(p, m)$. Function D is called demand. Unlike utility, demand is observed and, therefore, is better used to measure the well-being of the consumer. Key question is, is the consumer better or worse off when prices and income change? Let the price vector change from p to p' and income from m to m'. We are interested in an index of well-being, say $W(p, m)$, going up or down.

A first property that springs to mind is the following. If all prices and income are inflated by a common positive factor, say s, then the consumer will demand the same consumption bundle (as $spx \leq sm$ is equivalent to $px \leq m$), hence attain the same level of utility. In technical terms, as a function of prices and income, utility is homogeneous of degree zero. This was the situation when the euro was introduced. For example, in 1999 the Irish pound was replaced by $s = 1.27$ euros. All prices and income went up by 27%; consumers were not affected. It was also the situation when hyperinflation led to the reduction of zeros. For example, in 2009 Zimbabwe scrapped 12 zeros: $s = 10^{-12}$. The index of well-being should remain the same:

$$W(sp, sm) = W(p, m) \quad \text{for any } s > 0. \tag{1.1}$$

In mathematical terms, (1.1) means that well-being must be homogeneous of degree zero. Economically, condition (1.1) is absence of money illusion. However simple, we will see that most consumer's well-being measures found in the literature fail to meet *homogeneity test* (1.1).

A second property is the following. When the price vector changes from p to p' and income from m to m', demand will change from $D(p, m)$ to $D(p', m')$ and, therefore, utility from $U(D(p, m))$ to $U(D(p', m'))$. The composite function (of first demand and then utility) is called the indirect utility function and denoted by V. Formally, *indirect utility* is defined by $V(p, m) = U(D(p, m))$. We say that an index of well-being *tracks utility* when the consumer is measured as better off, $W(p, m) > W(p', m')$, if and only if the consumer is self-perceived as being better off, $V(p, m) > V(p', m')$.

There is a useful connection between the homogeneity test and the utility tracking property. Passing the homogeneity test is a necessary condition for utility tracking.

Proposition 1.1. *A well-being index tracks utility only if it passes the homogeneity test.*

Proof. The proof of this statement is by contradiction: Suppose an index tracks utility but does not meet the homogeneity test (1.1). Then there are p, m, and s with $W(sp, sm) \neq W(p, m)$. Hence, either $W(sp, sm) < W(p, m)$ or $W(sp, sm) > W(p, m)$. By utility tracking either $V(sp, sm) < V(p, m)$ or $V(sp, sm) > V(p, m)$. Hence, $V(sp, sm) \neq V(p, m)$. But this violates the property that indirect utility is homogeneous of degree zero. $\square$

The central well-being measure analyzed in this monograph is consumer's surplus, the difference between the value of commodities a consumer is willing to pay and the price (Marshall, 1920). Samuelson (1947, pp. 197–202) considered the uses of the concept. First, it is proposed as a measure of the gain (loss) of utility that results from a decrease (increase) in price of a single good. Second, it has been used as a measure of the burden involved in commodity taxation. Third, it has been used to determine the maximum amount of revenue that a perfectly discriminating monopolist might exact from the consumer for a given amount of the good in question. The utility tracking property is closely related to these uses, especially the first one. However, consumer's surplus will be shown to fail the homogeneity test (1.1) (in Chapter 6). It follows, by Proposition 1.1, that consumer's surplus does not track utility. A challenge is to modify the measure of consumer's surplus such that it tracks utility, and this monograph takes up the task.

This monograph is organized as follows. In Chapter 2, we review the theory of the consumer in microeconomics. The so-called expenditure function will be introduced. It will play a key role in the development and analysis of all well-being measures and price indices in this monograph.

Chapter 3 introduces the well-known equivalent and compensating variations. When the prices of one or several commodities increase, an important question is, what does this mean in terms of the price level, especially when wages are indexed? One way to measure this is to express the price increases in an equivalent reduction of income. Another way is to determine the income supplement that would compensate the price increases. The two measures are related but different. Chapter 4 introduces a compromise measure, called consumer's surplus. It measures the well-being of the consumer by the difference between the willingness to pay and pay. It is the most popular measure, because of its intuitive interpretation and the relative simplicity of its calculation. It is in between the equivalent and compensating variations.

Chapter 5 presents the constant elasticity of substitution utility and demand functions, the most popular ones in applied economics. Yet, surprisingly, it was only recently that the consumer's surplus formula for constant elasticity of substitution functions was found. It will be discussed in detail. Chapter 6 will test if well-being measures track utility. Chapter 7 shows the correspondence between these measures and price indices.

Chapters 8 and 9 are innovative. They present a new measure of consumer's well-being that, unlike the popular ones, has the desirable properties of homogeneity and utility tracking. There is a close connect with the theory of aggregation. Variants of the consumer's index are presented, including ones that are applicable to demand functions with income effects, even nonlinear ones. Even so-called broad measures of consumer well-being, such as the Human Development Index, will be encompassed. Chapter 10 concludes the monograph.

This monograph is the outgrowth of my recent work on consumer's surplus, in the context of homothetic demands. This contains some mind-boggling results, particularly the superiority of consumer's surplus vis-à-vis the equivalent and compensating variations, but when I attempted to extend the results to nonhomothetic demands, I decided to encompass the literature on demand aggregation and Divisia indices. As a result, the book has become a mixture of an introduction to the measurement of consumer's well-being and a review of advanced demand theory, particularly in Chapters 8 and 9. The mixture has the advantage of making the presentation self-contained and yet opening difficult issues, which, moreover, are often confused in the literature, such as the nature of path independence in the measurement of consumer's surplus and the Slutsky conditions, and, related, the permission or exclusion of income effects implicit in the use of consumer's surplus. It is hard to sort these issues, because of the overload of papers on consumer's surplus, most economic-theoretical, some excessively technical. The overload has snowed under some papers, such as Stahl's (1983) difficult yet important work on the Divisia index and Takayama's (1982) easier but lengthy work on consumer's surplus. Last, but not least, I will explore some exciting new directions, such as the extension of economic consumer well-being indices to other attributes, the area of broad well-being measures.

Chapter 2

The Theory of the Consumer in Microeconomics

In this chapter, we rush through the formal framework of the consumer, as provided by neoclassical economic theory, including simple, short proofs of the well-known formulas, Shephard's lemma, Slutsky equation, and Roy's lemma.

Goods and services are listed from 1 to n. A consumer consumes quantities $x_1, \ldots, x_n$, respectively, and we stack these quantities in vector x, the so-called consumption bundle. The consumer thus receives utility $U(x)$, which, however, is not observed. The prices of the goods and services are given by $p_1, \ldots, p_n$, and the available budget is m. All quantities, prices, and the budget are nonnegative numbers. The expenditure is $px = p_1x_1 + \cdots + p_nx_n$, where p is the price (row) vector. The budget set is the set of all commodity bundles x fulfilling $px \leq m$. The consumer selects the best available bundle, that is with the greatest utility, by solving the so-called problem of the consumer:

$$\max_x U(x) : px \leq m \qquad (2.1)$$

The solution to problem (2.1) is denoted $x = D(p, m)$, where D stands for *demand*, and carries utility $u = U(D(p, m))$. For simplicity, we make the technical assumption that utility is twice continuously differentiable, and the assumption that demand is

11

strictly quasi-concave. Then demand can be obtained by differentiation and will be unique for each price–budget combination; moreover, demand will be continuously differentiable. Solution $x = D(p, m)$ not only maximizes utility on the budget set, but also minimizes expenditure on the so-called better set:

$$\min_{x} px : U(x) \geq u \qquad (2.2)$$

There is one qualifier for the solution to fulfill (2.2), namely that utility is locally nonsatiated, which means that every neighborhood of any consumption bundle contains a bundle with higher utility. The proof that $x = D(p, m)$ fulfills (2.2) is by contradiction and runs as follows. If $x = D(p, m)$ does not solve (2.2), then there is an x' with $U(x') \geq u$ but $px' < px = pD(p, m)$. By local nonsatiation, any neighborhood of x' contains a bundle x'' with $U(x'') > u$. Select the neighborhood sufficiently small so that $px'' \leq pD(p, m)$, Then x'' contradicts that $u = U(x)$ is the optimum value of (2.1). This proves that the solution to (2.1), $x = D(p, m)$ solves (2.2) as well.

The parameters in problem (2.2) are price p and utility level u. Problem (2.2) determines how much expenditure is needed to attain a certain standard of living, u. The solution is denoted $e(p, u)$, where e stands for *expenditure* function.

An important class of utility functions consists of linearly homogeneous functions. Function U is linearly homogeneous if for every vector x and positive scalar s we have $U(sx) = sU(x)$. So, if the quantities are doubled, so will be the utility. Utility, quantities and, therefore, expenditures will all be proportionate. In (2.1) the quantities will be proportional to the budget m:

$$x = D(p, m) = D(p, 1)m \qquad (2.3)$$

Equation (2.3) holds for linearly homogeneous utility and implies two related equations, namely

$$U(D(p, m)) = mU(D(p, 1)) \qquad (2.4)$$

and, from (2.2),

$$e(p, u) = e(p, 1)u \qquad (2.5)$$

Equation (2.5) shows that expenditure is proportional to the standard of living and the coefficient, $e(p, 1)$, is a function of price. Here, $e(p, 1)$ is a price index. When components of price vector p change, so that p turns p', the expenditure required to maintain the standard of living, u, grows by the factor $e(p', 1)/e(p, 1)$. This change of the cost-of-living index is independent of u, by the assumed linear homogeneity of utility. However, results (2.4) and (2.5) can be extended to nonlinearly homogeneous functions, as will be discussed now.

By definition, a *homogeneous* function fulfills $U(sx) = s^d U(x)$, where $d > 0$ is the degree of homogeneity. Such utility functions are monotonic transformations of each other and hence equivalent in terms of the problem of the consumer, (2.1). Equations (2.4) and (2.5) show that utility and expenditure are multiplicatively separable in each other and the price. Their mutual dependence is linear and the dependence on price is nonlinear. A further monotonic transformation renders the separability additive. The transformation that does the trick is the natural logarithm. So consider $\ln U$ with $U(sx) = sU(x)$. By equations (2.3) and (2.4), we see that $\ln U(D(p, m)) = \ln U(D(p, 1)m) = \ln[mU(D(p, 1))] = \ln U(D(p, 1)) + \ln m$. We see that $\ln U$ is additively separable in price and budget.

Additive separability is common in industry studies. The welfare contribution is measured by, e.g. the sum of the consumer's surplus generated by the industry products and the residual budget, spent on other products. This monograph, however, will slightly revise the concept of consumer's surplus and argue that a better measure of welfare is based on multiplicative separability.

The generalization to nonlinear homogeneity is completed as follows. Functions which are a monotonic transformation of a homogeneous function are called *homothetic*. If utility is homothetic, we may continue to use equations (2.4) and (2.5).

Throughout this book we will use Shephard's lemma and Roy's lemma. They follow from equations (2.1) and (2.2) for general utility functions, not necessarily homothetic. Shephard's lemma is a formula for the derivative of the expenditure function. It will be used to set up the Hicksian measures of consumer's well-being. It is also used to prove Roy's lemma, which expresses demand in terms of indirect utility, defined in Chapter 1. Roy's lemma is used to derive demand functions and utility tracking measures of well-being. Simple derivations of the lemmas are as follows.

Recall that the parameters in expenditure problem (2.2) are price p and utility level u, and that the solution value is denoted by $e(p, u)$. The bundle that costs this amount of money depends on the parameters of the problem, hence is a function of p and $u : x = D^c(p, u)$. Function D^c is called *compensated demand*. It traces the response of the consumer to price changes when the standard of living, u, is maintained, by budgetary compensation. Shephard's lemma will state that the derivative of the expenditure function with respect to price, $\frac{\partial e}{\partial p}$, equals compensated demand. Since p is a price vector, $\frac{\partial e}{\partial p}$ is a vector, with components $\frac{\partial e}{\partial p_1}, \ldots, \frac{\partial e}{\partial p_n}$. It is customary to consider $\frac{\partial e}{\partial p}$ a row vector. This eases the differentiation of vectors, such as $\frac{\partial D_1}{\partial p}, \ldots, \frac{\partial D_n}{\partial p}$. These are now n row vectors which can be stacked in a matrix, denoted $\frac{\partial D}{\partial p}$. Similarly, we have matrix $\frac{\partial D^c}{\partial p}$. The latter matrix has the following important and powerful property. If utility is locally nonsatiated, then

$$p\frac{\partial D^c}{\partial p} = 0^{\mathrm{T}} \tag{2.6}$$

As a preliminary to the proof, note that the left-hand side of equation (2.6) is the product of a row vector and a matrix.

Therefore, the right-hand side must also be a row vector. Indeed, the transposition sign T turns column vector 0 (all components are scalar 0) into a row vector.

The proof of equation (2.6) is as follows. By local non-satiation, the constraint in (2.2) is binding: $U(D^c(p, u)) = u$. Differentiating with respect to price, the chain rule yields $\left(\frac{\partial U}{\partial x}\right)^{\mathrm{T}} \frac{\partial D^c}{\partial p} = 0^{\mathrm{T}}$. For non-corner solutions, the first-order condition of problem (2.2) is that the derivative of the objective function is proportional to the derivative of the constraint function: $p = \lambda \left(\frac{\partial U}{\partial x}\right)^{\mathrm{T}}$, where λ is the Lagrange multiplier (the well-known condition that the marginal utilities are proportional to the prices). Substitution and division by λ (which is positive by local nonsatiation) completes the proof of equation (2.6) for non-corner solutions. The extension to corner solutions is by the phenomenon of complementary slackness for nondegenerate program (2.2): (2.6) holds true for the non-corner solutions and D^c remains 0 locally for the corner solutions using the assumption of twice continuously differentiable utility.

An immediate consequence of equation (2.6) is

Shephard's lemma: *If utility is locally nonsatiated, then* $\frac{\partial e}{\partial p}(p, u) = D^c(p, u)$.

Proof: Using local nonsatiation the expenditure is $e(p, u) = pD^c(p, u)$. Differentiating with respect to price, the left-hand side yields the left-hand side of Shephard's lemma, while the right-hand side yields, using the product rule, $D^c(p, u) + p\frac{\partial}{\partial p}D^c(p, u)$. Here, the second term vanishes by equation (2.6). This completes the proof of Shephard's lemma. Strictly speaking $\frac{\partial e}{\partial p}$ is a row vector, hence must be transposed in Roy's lemma, but this is not customary and confusion does not arise. □

Shephard's lemma has two important consequences, namely the Slutsky equation and Roy's lemma. The Slutsky equation decomposes price effects on demand in a substitution term and an income term; it will prove useful in constructing a price index (Chapter 7).

Slutsky equation: If utility is locally nonsatiated, then $\frac{\partial D}{\partial p} = \frac{\partial D^c}{\partial p} - \frac{\partial D}{\partial m} D^{\mathrm{T}}$.

The (i,j)th element of the Slutsky equation reads $\frac{\partial D_i}{\partial p_j} = \frac{\partial D_i^c}{\partial p_j} - \frac{\partial D_i}{\partial m} D_j$. Since the last term must also constitute a matrix, the last term of Slutsky equation is written as the product of a column vector, $\frac{\partial D}{\partial m}$, and a row vector, D^{T}. This explains the transposition sign in the Slutsky equation.

Proof: The fact that $x = D(p,m)$ solves (2.2) (assuming local nonsatiation) means that $D^c(p,u) = D(p,e(p,u))$. Differentiating with respect to price, $\frac{\partial D^c}{\partial p} = \frac{\partial D}{\partial p} + \frac{\partial D}{\partial m}\frac{\partial e}{\partial p}$. Substitution of Shephard's lemma and $D^c(p,u) = D(p,e(p,u))$ yields the Slutsky equation. $\qquad\square$

A well-known aspect of the Slutsky equation is *Slutsky symmetry*: $\frac{\partial D}{\partial p} + \frac{\partial D}{\partial m} D^{\mathrm{T}}$ is a symmetric matrix. The reason is that it equals $\frac{\partial D^c}{\partial p}$ (by the Slutsky equation) hence $\frac{\partial^2 e}{\partial p^2}$ (by Shephard's lemma). Since the order of taking second partial derivatives does not matter when they are continuous, by the theorem of Schwarz (1873), the matrix is symmetric indeed. Slutsky symmetry will play a role in the concept of consumer's surplus and the variants proposed in this book.

Roy's lemma is about indirect utility $V(p,m)$; it will be used extensively to derive demand functions and to determine consumer's surplus. The formal statement is as follows.

Roy's lemma: *If utility is locally nonsatiated, then* $D(p,m) = -\frac{\partial V}{\partial p} / \frac{\partial V}{\partial m}$.

Proof: Denote the level of indirect utility, $V(p,m) = U(D(p,m))$, by u, then $V(p,m) = u$. By local nonsatiation the required amount of money to attain u is $m = e(p,u)$. Then

$D(p, m) = D^c(p, u)$ and $V(p, e(p, u)) = u$. Differentiate the last equation with respect to price. By the chain rule, $\frac{\partial V}{\partial p} + \frac{\partial V}{\partial m} \frac{\partial e}{\partial p} = 0$. Substitution of Shephard's lemma and $D(p, m) = D^c(p, u)$ yields the desired result. $\qquad\square$

Strictly speaking $\frac{\partial V}{\partial p}$ is a row vector, hence must be transposed in Roy's lemma, but this is not customary. In the interest of a simple exposition, consider a price increase of just one good, from scalar p to scalar p'. All the other prices remain fixed, for example, at unity. Denote the demand and compensated demand for the good of which the price changes by scalars $D(p, m)$ and $D^c(p, u)$. Strictly speaking there should be subscripts indicating the commodity under consideration, but we omit them in analyzing the demand for the good under consideration. This abuse of notation suggests that the analysis will remain valid in the general case where p and $D(p)$ are vectors, and that is rightly so. The price increase reduces the budget set. The compensated demand function, however, is based on a greater budget. We expect that after the price increase the compensated demand is stronger than the ordinary demand, but that is true only if the good is a normal good. By definition, a good is *normal* if the demand increases with income. The situation for a normal good is depicted in Figure 2.1.

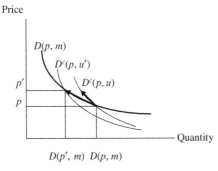

Figure 2.1 A price increase from p to p' lowers demand. A compensated demand curve runs through each demand point.

In Figure 2.1, we adopt the convention of economists, due to Marshall (1920), of plotting the independent variable, that is price, along the vertical axis. Figure 2.1 illustrates that when the price goes up from p to p', then both demand and compensated demand are reduced, but compensated demand remains relatively sizable. This explains why the compensated demand curve is steeper than the ordinary demand curve. The two shifts are indicated by the two arrows in Figure 2.1. In the new situation utility will be smaller, say u', and another compensated demand function can be drawn, indexed by $D^c(p, u')$. Compensated demand is a function of p and u, hence for each u we have a compensated demand curve. The compensated demand curves have been introduced by Hicks (1942) who used them to measure the effect of a price change on the well-being of the consumer, by means of his compensating and equivalent variations. Since these measures enjoy authority in the literature, which will be questioned in this book, and lead me to propose alternative, superior measures, it is important to analyze the Hicksian measures in detail. They are presented in the next chapter.

Chapter 3

Hicksian Measures: Equivalent and Compensating Variations

The equivalent variation and the compensating variation are exact, monetary measures for the loss of purchasing power that consumers experience when prices change. The equivalent variation measures the reduction of the consumer's budget that is equivalent to a given price increase — that is, the amount of money that could have been taken from the consumer instead of increasing the price. A close cousin of the equivalent variation is the compensating variation; it measures the increase in the consumer's budget that compensates for the effect of a price increase. In other words, the compensating variation is the amount of money that would have to be given to the consumer to maintain the standard of living after a price increase. The determination of the compensating variation rests on an analysis of the consumer under the new price regime. The two measures are related and will be used in Chapter 4 as the basis for a practical compromise: the evaluation of consumer's well-being by means of consumer's surplus.

Consider a price change from vector p to vector p'. Think of an increase in just one price component. Utility will go down, from u to u'. Had the prices not changed, the same reduction of the living standard could have been achieved by reducing the budget from m to $e(p, u')$.

Definition: The *equivalent variation* of the price change from p to p' is $E = m - e(p, u')$.

A reduction of the budget by this amount would reduce the standard of living as much as the price change from p to p' does. Hence, the equivalent variation is a level measure for the change in the prices. The reference point is the base situation, with price p. One can also use the new situation, with prices given by p', as a reference point. Then the question is the following. In the new situation, how much subsidy is needed to restore the old standard of living?

Definition: The *compensating variation* of the price change from p to p' is $C = e(p', u) - m$.

A subsidy of this amount would allow the consumer to maintain the standard of living, u, under the new price regime, p'. The compensating variation is an alternative level measure for the change in the prices. For a price increase, money will become less valuable and, therefore, we expect the compensating variation to be greater than the equivalent variation.

The two measures have graphical interpretations, as will be shown now. Let us begin with the equivalent variation, $m - e(p, u')$. In the new situation, with prices given by p', budget m buys you only utility u', with u' determined by the equation $m = e(p', u')$, assuming local nonsatiation. Hence, the equivalent variation equals

$$E = e(p', u') - e(p, u') \tag{3.1}$$

Equation (3.1) equals the line integral $\int_p^{p'} \frac{\partial e(p'', u')}{\partial p} dp''$, or, by Shephard's lemma (Chapter 2), $\int_p^{p'} D^c(p'', u') dp''$. In other words, the equivalent variation amounts the area 'under' the compensated demand curve associated with the new (low) utility level, u'. I write 'under' as in the Marshallian tradition, see Figures 2.1 or 3.1, price is along the vertical axis and the area

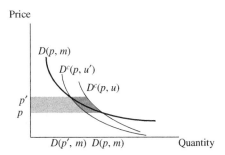

Figure 3.1 The equivalent variation is represented by the lightly shaded area to the left-hand side of the new compensated demand curve $D^c(p, u')$. The compensating variation is represented by the same area plus the darker shaded area to the left-hand side of the original compensated demand curve $D^c(p, u)$.

is thus to the left of the compensated demand curve. Likewise, the compensating variation $e(p', u) - m$ equals

$$C = e(p', u) - e(p, u) \qquad (3.2)$$

Equation (3.2) equals the line integral $\int_p^{p'} D^c(p'', u)dp''$, the area 'under' the compensated demand curve associated with the old (high) utility level, u. Figure 3.1 shows these findings for a normal good, for which demand increases with income (Chapter 2).

These findings confirm our intuition that the compensating variation is greater than the equivalent variation, for normal goods. They also suggest that these measures fail the homogeneity test, (1.1), simply because the areas that represent them grow when the monetary unit of measurement shrinks, and, therefore, do not track utility (Proposition 1.1).

For illustration and future critical discussion of the two measures, let us work out a simple example. Consider Cobb–Douglas utility $u(x_1, x_2) = \frac{1}{2} \ln x_1 + \frac{1}{2} \ln x_2$ and let the prices be 1 and 1. Maximizing utility, the consumer will split his budget, let it be one dollar, between the two goods, so that $x_1 = x_2 = \frac{1}{2}$. Now let the price of x_1 almost triple; more precisely, let it be increased by a factor e, where e is Euler's number, which is (2.72) rounded. The consumer will still split his budget, but now $ex_1 = x_2 = \frac{1}{2}$. Hence, $x_1 = 1/(2e)$ and $x_2 = \frac{1}{2}$. Utility goes down from $\ln \frac{1}{2}$ to $\ln \frac{1}{2} - \frac{1}{2}$.

The consumer is worse off, but by how much? Well, the new, low level of utility could also have been achieved by imposing a tax E such that the new utility level is attained. The consumer would split his budget, $x_1 = x_2 = \frac{1}{2}(1 - E)$, getting utility $\ln[\frac{1}{2}(1 - E)]$. E is the equivalent variation. In fact,

$$E = 1 - 1/\sqrt{e} = 0.39 \tag{3.3}$$

because then $\ln[\frac{1}{2}(1 - E)] = \ln(\frac{1}{2}/\sqrt{e}) = \ln \frac{1}{2} - \frac{1}{2}$.

Alternatively, the consumer can be given a subsidy C such that his utility is restored to the old level, $\ln \frac{1}{2}$. The consumer will split his budget, $ex_1 = x_2 = \frac{1}{2} + \frac{1}{2}C$, getting utility $\ln(\frac{1}{2} + \frac{1}{2}C) - \frac{1}{2}$. C is the compensating variation. In fact,

$$C = \sqrt{e} - 1 = 0.65 \tag{3.4}$$

because then $\frac{1}{2}\ln\{[(\frac{1}{2} + \frac{1}{2}(\sqrt{e} - 1)]/e\} - \frac{1}{2}\ln[(\frac{1}{2} + \frac{1}{2}(\sqrt{e} - 1)] = \ln(\frac{1}{2}\sqrt{e}) - \frac{1}{2} = \ln \frac{1}{2}$, the old utility level. Indeed, $C > E$, as the reference point is the new, high price situation, so that you need more money to maintain utility.

A well-known, useful result is the connection between the equivalent and compensating variations. We considered a change from p to p'. By equation (3.1), the equivalent variation is $E = e(p', u') - e(p, u')$. If we swap the initial situation (unprimed) and the new situation (primed), looking backward instead of forward, we obtain $e(p, u) - e(p', u)$. By equation (3.2), this is minus the compensating variation. If a price goes up, the equivalent variation is minus the compensating variation associated with the price reduction looking backward. The equivalent variation and the compensating variation are twins. This observation has several interesting implications. In price index theory an axiom is that if the price system goes back and forth, the price level remains the same. This does not happen if the index is based only on the equivalent variation or only on the compensating variation. For example, in the just considered Cobb–Douglas case, with the price of good 1 rising from 1 to e, equation (3.3) shows that $E = 0.39$. Now consider the price changes from e to 1. Then utility goes from u' to u and, applying equation (3.1) with the roles of p and p' reversed and hence of u and u' reversed as well, the equivalent variation in the price reversal is $e(p, u) - e(p', u)$. But this amount equals $-C$ according to the equation, which is -0.65 by equation (3.4). Hence, the price level goes up 39 cents and down 65 cents. The total effect is not zero. Since the compensating variation is the mirror image of the equivalent variation, it has the same flaw. The critiques will be articulated in Chapter 6.

So far income was presumed to be constant, but it is straightforward to accommodate an income change in the Hicksian measures. When a price goes up, expenditure goes up. The equivalent variation, E, and the compensating variation, C, will be positive, see equations (3.1) and (3.2). The effect of the price increase is an increase in the cost of living, be it measured by E or C. The standard of living is reduced. This explains why we insert negative signs when measuring the standard of living. Thus, if at the same time the budget goes up from m to m', an increase of $m' - m$, the net effect on the standard of living is $m' - m - E$ or, using the compensating variation, $m' - m - C$. Substituting equation (3.1), $m = e(p, u)$ and $m' = e(p', u')$ (assuming local nonsatiation), the *equivalent variation-based standard of living measure* is

$$m' - m - [e(p', u') - e(p, u')] = e(p, u') - e(p, u) \qquad (3.5)$$

Equation (3.5) shows that the equivalent variation-based standard of living measure equals the increase in monetary utility, that is expressed by the expenditure function, at price p. Likewise, substituting equation (3.2), $m = e(p, u)$ and $m' = e(p', u')$ (assuming local nonsatiation), the *compensating variation-based standard of living measure* reads

$$m' - m - [e(p', u) - e(p, u)] = e(p', u') - e(p', u) \qquad (3.6)$$

Equation (3.6) shows that the compensating variation-based standard of living measure equals the increase in monetary utility, that is expressed by the expenditure function, at price p'.

The drawback of these standard of living measures is that they are not invariant with respect to the monetary unit, a recurrent theme in this book. Fortunately, there is an easy fix, namely to take the logarithms of expenditure or, equivalently, to take the ratio of the expenditures, instead of the differences. Thus, the equivalent variation-based standard of living measure is $e(p, u')/e(p, u)$ and, likewise, the compensating variation-based standard of living measure is $e(p', u')/e(p', u)$. Jorgenson's (1990) measure of the standard of living is the first one, hence, equivalent variation-based.

A first compromise between the equivalent variation and the compensating variation is consumer's surplus, the subject of the next chapter. Not surprisingly, consumer's surplus will inherit the flaws of the equivalent compensating variations — in fact, most economists believe consumer's surplus is a worse measure — but, and this is surprising, it will prove to have an advantage. Consumer's surplus will be the basis of improved measures to be developed in Chapters 6, 8, and 9.

Chapter 4

Marshallian Measure: Consumer's Surplus

The equivalent and compensating variations are well defined methods of measuring the effect of a price change in terms of money, but there are two practical problems with this approach. First, the measures differ, so it is not clear which one to use. Second, calculating the two measures requires Hicksian compensated demand functions, which are unobserved. An answer to these issues is consumer's surplus. The difference between the equivalent and compensating variations is the dark shaded area in Figure 3.1, between the two compensated demand functions and the two price lines. This is true whether the good affected by the price change is normal or not. The dark shaded difference area is intersected by the ordinary demand function. The compromise between the two shaded areas, one left of the compensated demand function on the left and the other left of the compensated demand function on the right, is the area left of the ordinary demand function, between the price lines that represent the old and the new price situations. The area measures the variation of consumer's surplus, a concept that will be explained next. The choice of this measure kills two birds with one stone. The measure settles the issue of difference between the equivalent and compensating variations, and it replaces unobserved compensated demand functions by an observed ordinary demand function.

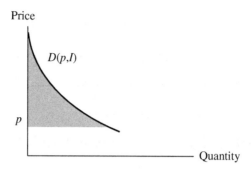

Figure 4.1 At price p, the consumer's surplus is the area between the price line (the lower boundary of the shaded area) and the demand curve.

Figure 4.1 plots the demand curve for a given budget, m. Because of the Marshallian convention of plotting quantity along the horizontal axis, it plots price as a function of quantity of the goods demanded by the consumer. This is the inverse demand function — also called the willingness-to-pay function.

Figure 4.1 shows the quantity of the good demanded when the price is p. The price the consumer pays for all units of the good is reduced as he buys more units. For example, if he pays 1¢ per unit for 10 units but only 0.99¢ per unit when he buys 11 units, he earns one cent on each of the first 10 units and adds 10 cents to his overall consumer's surplus. The difference between the consumer's willingness-to-pay and the price is therefore called consumer's surplus; it is represented by the shaded area in Figure 4.1.

Definition: *Consumer's surplus* is the integral of the demand function from the prices p to infinity

$$CS(p, m) = \int_p^\infty D(p', m) dp' \tag{4.1}$$

In equation (4.1) p is a price vector and $D(p, m)$ is a quantity vector, and we use the following notation, $D(p, m) dp = D_1(p, m) dp_1 + \cdots + D_n(p, m) dp_n$. Should only one price change, say p_i, then all of the other terms in the sum will be zero and all that remains under the integral sign $\int$ in definition (4.1) is $D(p, m)\, dp = D_i(p, m)\, dp_i$.

A price change from p to p' reduces consumer's surplus by the following amount:

$$S = CS(p, m) - CS(p', m)$$

$$= \int_p^\infty D(p'', m)\, dp'' - \int_{p'}^\infty D(p'', m)\, dp'' = \int_p^{p'} D(p'', m)\, dp''$$

$$(4.2)$$

Reduction S in equation (4.2) is called the *variation of consumer's surplus* and represents the compromise between the equivalent variation and the compensating variation denoted in Figure 3.1. Like the latter two, the variation of consumer's surplus measures the reduction of consumer's well-being that accompanies price increases. It has the advantage that it is based on the ordinary demand function, which can be estimated using sales data.

Income is fixed in equation (4.2). If income also changes, from m to m', then the *variation of consumer's surplus* will be defined by $CS(p, m) - CS(p', m')$.

A handy formula for analyzing the reduction of consumer's surplus resulting from a price increase is the following. Equation (4.1) shows that consumer's surplus is the integral of ordinary demand, given as a function of price. Since integration is differentiation in reverse, the *derivative of consumer's surplus with respect to price is equal to demand*:

$$\frac{\partial}{\partial p} CS(p, m) = -D(p, m) \qquad (4.3)$$

The negative sign in equation (4.3) reflects the fact that consumer's surplus is reduced when the price of a good increases.

Mathematically, this stems from the fact that variable p is in the *lower* bound of integral (4.1).

Let us return to the example of Chapter 3, where utility is given by the Cobb–Douglas function $u(x_1, x_2) = \frac{1}{2}\ln x_1 + \frac{1}{2}\ln x_2$, the prices are 1 and 1, with the first price changing to Euler's number e, rounded 2.72, and where the budget is $m = 1$. Demand changed from $x_1 = x_2 = \frac{1}{2}$ to $x_1 = 1/(2e)$, $x_2 = \frac{1}{2}$ and utility changed from $\ln\frac{1}{2}$ to $\ln\frac{1}{2} - \frac{1}{2}$. The area under the demand curve, $x_1 = 1/(2p_1)$ — of which the integral is $\frac{1}{2}\ln p_1$ — between the old price 1 and the new price e, is, by equation (4.2), $S = \frac{1}{2}\ln e - \frac{1}{2}\ln 1$. Hence,

$$S = 0.50 \qquad (4.4)$$

The variation of consumer's surplus S was defined in (4.2) as the *reduction* of consumer's surplus. This gives it the same (positive) sign as of E and V of (3.3) and (3.4). In fact, the variation of consumer's surplus is in between the equivalent variation and the compensating variation values, provided demand is normal.

The equivalent and compensating variations as well as consumer's surplus all express the effect of a price increase in terms of money. Now let us address the question how they measure up to a budget change. We analyze the change in consumer economic well-being when price and income change simultaneously, with an unfavorable change in price and a favorable change in the budget. We keep the same Cobb–Douglas example — the price of commodity 1 increases from 1 to e — but now consider three alternative budget increases, namely from $1 to $m = \$1.39$, from $1 to 1.50, and from $1 to 1.65. The respective budget increases coincide with the equivalent variation (E), the variation of consumer's surplus (S), and the compensating variation (C), according to equations (3.3), (4.4), and (3.4). For each scenario, Table 4.1 displays the utility change

Table 4.1 The combined impacts of a price increase from 1 to e and a budget change from 1 to 1.39, 1.50, or 1.65 on utility and on three monetary measures.

New budget	Δutility	Δbudget – E	Δbudget – S	Δbudget – C
1.39	−0.17	0	−0.11	−0.26
1.50	−0.09	0.11	0	−0.15
1.65	0	0.26	0.15	0

and the three monetary proxies to assess the combined price–budget change.

The second column in Table 4.1 requires the computation of indirect utility. In the new situation, the consumer maximizes $u(x_1, x_2) = \frac{1}{2}\ln x_1 + \frac{1}{2}\ln x_2$ subject to $ex_1 + x_2 \le m$. The consumer splits the budget, $ex_1 = x_2 = m/2$, hence, $u = \frac{1}{2}\ln(\frac{1}{2}m/e) + \frac{1}{2}\ln(\frac{1}{2}m) = \ln \frac{1}{2} + \ln m - \frac{1}{2}\ln e$. The last two terms, or briefly $\ln m - \frac{1}{2}$, imply the change in utility.

Let us review the three alternative measures in Table 4.1, Δbudget – E, Δbudget – S, and Δbudget – C. The first measure overestimates the change in utility in all three new budget cases, even just in terms of sign, which is all that is relevant for ordinal utility. The second measure overestimates the change in utility in two cases, in terms of sign. The third measure correctly estimates the change in utility, in terms of sign. We might be tempted to deduce that budget increase minus compensating variation is the candidate for the best measure, but this is false. From Chapter 3, we know that if an equivalent variation-based measure has a flaw, such as the overestimation in sign in Table 4.1, then the compensating variation-based measure has the same flaw. This can be supported by an example like in Table 4.1.

An important issue that plagues consumer's surplus is the path dependence of its defining integral, especially when income changes as well. For small, infinitesimal changes in price consumer's surplus is fine; its variation is well defined and tracks utility. This is shown by analyzing the problem of the consumer, $\max_x U(x) : px \leq m$ (2.1). The Lagrangian function is $U(x) + \lambda(m-px)$ where λ is the Lagrange multiplier, which measures the marginal utility of the bound of the constraint, money m. In fact, $du = \lambda(dm - x \cdot dp)$, where the dot is the inner product. Dividing through by λ, which is positive assuming local nonsatiation,

$$-D(p,m)dp + dm = du/\lambda \qquad (4.5)$$

Equation (4.5) shows that for infinitesimal price and income changes the sum of the variations in consumer's surplus and the budget measures the variation of utility. This result extends to larger price and income changes if utility is homothetic. This will be shown now for linearly homogeneous utility, which suffices (as homothetic utility is a monotonic transformation of a homogeneous function). Setting the derivative of the Lagrangian function equal to zero, we have the well-known first-order condition $\frac{\partial U(x)}{\partial x} = \lambda p$. Hence, $x\frac{\partial U(x)}{\partial x} = \lambda px = \lambda m$. By Euler's theorem this simplifies to $U(x) = \lambda m$. In other words, utility is a linear function of money and, therefore, λ, the marginal utility of money, is constant. The reasoning can also be reversed. If $U(x) = \lambda m$, then differentiating $U(x) = \lambda px$ we have $\frac{\partial U(x)}{\partial x} = \lambda p$ and, therefore, $\frac{\partial U(x)}{\partial x}x = \lambda px = U(x)$, which by Euler's theorem implies that U is linearly homogeneous. Invoking a monotonic transformation, we obtain the result that the marginal utility of money is constant if and only if utility is homothetic (Lau, 1970).

It follows that if utility is homothetic, the change in utility as (p, m) changes to (p', m') is given by the line integral of the left-hand side of equation (4.5). The right-hand side becomes the change in utility $u' - u$, apart from factor $1/\lambda$, which is constant. The second term on the left-hand side becomes the change in money, $m' - m$. Integrating with respect to price the leading term of (4.5) becomes, using equation (4.3) and the cancellation of two minus signs, $\int_p^{p'} \frac{\partial}{\partial p} CS(p'', m) dp'' = CS(p', m) - CS(p, m)$, i.e. the variation at consumer's surplus when income is m. In mathematical terms, the demand vector field is conservative with respect to price, and consumer's surplus is the scalar field that generates it; by the gradient theorem the line integral is path independent. Proposition 4.1 summarizes.

Proposition 4.1. *The variation of consumer's surplus measures welfare if utility is homothetic and income is constant.*

Proof. Since income is constant, $m = m'$, hence, (4.5) integrates to $u' - u = \lambda[CS(p', m) - CS(p, m)]$. $\qquad\square$

A neat application of consumer's surplus is an assessment of the benefit of the 130 ferry services in Norway. Jørgensen *et al.* (2011) have, for each ferry service, three sets of data for 2007, namely, x°, the number of vehicles transported by the ferry; p°, the fare for the ferry; and $-\varepsilon^\circ$, the elasticity of demand (derived from other information). Here superscript ∘ stands for 'observed.' The data fit a demand curve $D(p)$ (without an income argument). To be consistent with these data, curve D must have the right level and the right slope at price $p^\circ : D(p^\circ) = x^\circ$ and elasticity $[dD(p^\circ)/dp]/[D(p^\circ)/p^\circ] = -\varepsilon^\circ$. The authors postulate demand function $D(p) = x^\circ e^{\varepsilon^\circ(1-p/p^\circ)}$, which indeed fulfills these two consistency requirements. The first requirement, $D(p^\circ) = x^\circ$, is trivially fulfilled. And elasticity of demand $[dD(p)/dp]/[D(p)/p] = -(\varepsilon^\circ/p^\circ)p$ takes value $-\varepsilon^\circ$ at price p° In this example, consumer's surplus is proportional to sales, as we will see now. By definition (4.1) $CS(p) = \int_{p^\circ}^\infty x^\circ e^{\varepsilon^\circ(1-p/p^\circ)} dp = [x^\circ e^{\varepsilon^\circ(1-p/p^\circ)}/(\varepsilon^\circ/p^\circ)]_{p=p^\circ}^\infty = p^\circ x^\circ/\varepsilon^\circ$. This simplified benefit analysis requires only sales and elasticity figures. The sales figures are readily available, and the elasticities were already derived from the changes in demand that followed the reductions in ferry fares: -0.26, -0.35, and -0.46 for short, medium, and long ferry services, respectively. Substituting and summing yields a total consumer surplus of 725 million euros for these ferry service price reductions, or € 270 per vehicle (Statistics Norway reports that 2.7 million vehicles used Norway's ferry services in 2007).

What happens if income m changes, say to m'? Unfortunately, the line integral of the left-hand side of equation (4.5) now depends on the path of integration from (p, m) to (p', m'). For example, consider two rectangular paths of integration for (4.5): I. First change p to p', then change m to m'. And II. First change m to m', then change p to p'. The line integral becomes as follows.

Path I. The integral of (4.1) is $CS(p', m) - CS(p, m) + m' - m$.

Path II. The integral of (4.1) is $m' - m + CS(p', m') - CS(p, m')$.

By homotheticity, see (2.3) and (4.1), $CS(p, m) = CS(p, 1)m$. So the difference between the integrals along paths II and I becomes $[CS(p', 1) - CS(p, 1)](m' - m)$, which is nonzero if income changes. Consumer's surplus fails the homogeneity test, (1.1), because, as with the equivalent and compensating variations, the area that represents it grows when the monetary unit of measurement shrinks, and, therefore, consumer's surplus does not track utility (Proposition 1.1). We will have to modify the concept of variation of consumer's surplus to let it be a consumer's welfare measure that remains applicable when income changes.

The modification of consumer's surplus will be discussed in Chapter 6 for constant elasticity of substitution (CES) utility functions and then fixed in Chapters 8 and 9. Clearly, it is useful to first analyze CES functions, the subject of the next chapter.

Chapter 5

Constant Elasticity of Substitution Functions

An important class of utility functions are the constant elasticity of substitution (CES) functions, the workhorse of applied economics. The class encompasses Leontief's fixed coefficients functions and the fixed budget shares Cobb–Douglas functions. The formula of the CES function is

$$U(x_1, \ldots, x_n) = (\alpha_1 x_1^\rho + \cdots + \alpha_n x_n^\rho)^{1/\rho} \qquad (5.1)$$

The coefficients, $\alpha_1, \ldots, \alpha_n$, are nonnegative and may and will be assumed to *sum to one*. The adding-up constraint can be fulfilled by an increasing transformation of the utility function. The *elasticity of substitution* measures the sensitivity of the proportions of demand, such as x_1/x_2, with respect to relative price, p_1/p_2. Formally, it is defined by $\sigma = -\frac{\partial(x_1/x_2)/(x_1/x_2)}{\partial(p_1/p_2)/(p_1/p_2)}$, where the minus sign is included to make the elasticity of substitution nonnegative. Price does not show in equation (5.1), but the first-order condition of maximization of utility subject to a budget constraint is that the derivative of the objective function is proportional to the derivative of the constraint function: $\frac{\partial U}{\partial x} = \lambda p$, where λ is the Lagrange multiplier. This is the well-known condition that the marginal utilities are proportional to the prices. It follows that $p_2/p_1 = \frac{\partial U}{\partial x_2}/\frac{\partial U}{\partial x_1} = \alpha_2 x_2^{\rho-1}/\alpha_1 x_1^{\rho-1} = (\alpha_2/\alpha_1)(x_2/x_1)^{\rho-1}$, by application of the chain rule to (5.1). Solving,

$$x_2/x_1 = (\alpha_2/\alpha_1)^{1/(1-\rho)} (p_2/p_1)^{-1/(1-\rho)} \tag{5.2}$$

The elasticity of a power function, say $y = ax^c$, is $\frac{\partial y/y}{\partial x/x} = x(acx^{c-1})/(ax^c) = c$, i.e. the power. The power in (5.2) is $-1/(1-\rho)$, but by inclusion of the minus sign in the definition of elasticity substitution we have

$$\sigma = 1/(1-\rho) \tag{5.3}$$

Result (5.3) shows that function (5.1) has a constant elasticity of substitution indeed. We derived this result for the pair of commodities 1 and 2, but it holds for any pair. As we vary parameter ρ, the elasticity of substitution varies, in the same direction, as (5.3) features an increasing relationship. Several well-known utility functions are encompassed, see Table 5.1.

We must show that the three values of parameter ρ in column 3 of Table 5.1 reduce the CES formula to the special ones in column 2 of Table 5.1. For the linear function (see the bottom row of Table 5.1), this is done by simple substitution of $\rho = 1$ in the CES formula.

Table 5.1 Constant elasticity of substitution functions.

Function name	Formula $U(x_1,\ldots,x_n)$	Parameter ρ	Elasticity of substitution $\sigma = 1/(1-\rho)$
CES	$(\alpha_1 x_1^\rho + \cdots + \alpha_n x_n^\rho)^{1/\rho}$	≤ 1	≥ 0
Leontief	$\min(x_1,\ldots,x_n)$	$-\infty$	0
Cobb–Douglas	$x_1^{\alpha_1} \cdots x_n^{\alpha_n}$	0	1
Linear	$\alpha_1 x_1 + \cdots + \alpha_n x_n$	1	∞

For the Leontief function, we must do some work. CES
$U(x_1, \ldots, x_n) = (\alpha_1 x_1^\rho + \cdots + \alpha_n x_n^\rho)^{1/\rho} = \left[1 + \frac{\alpha_2}{\alpha_1}\left(\frac{x_2}{x_1}\right)^\rho + \cdots + \frac{\alpha_n}{\alpha_1}\left(\frac{x_n}{x_1}\right)^\rho\right]^{1/\rho}(\alpha_1 x_1^\rho)^{1/\rho} = \left[1 + \frac{\alpha_2}{\alpha_1}\left(\frac{x_1}{x_2}\right)^{-\rho} + \cdots + \frac{\alpha_n}{\alpha_1}\left(\frac{x_1}{x_n}\right)^{-\rho}\right]^{1/\rho}\alpha_1^{1/\rho}x_1$.
If $x_1 < x_2, \ldots, x_n$, then $\rho \to -\infty$ or $-\rho \to \infty$ implies that
$U(x_1, \ldots, x_n) \to [1 + 0 + \cdots + 0]^0 \alpha_1^0 x_1 = x_1 = \min(x_1, \ldots, x_n)$
and we obtain similar results if the minimum is assumed by
$x_2, \ldots,$ or x_n.

Table 5.1 features a special case of the Leontief function, with
coefficients 1. Yet, it encompasses the general Leontief function.
Had we started with a slightly more general CES function,
featuring $x_1/a_1, \ldots, x_n/a_n$ instead of $x_1, \ldots, x_n$, then we would
have obtained the standard Leontief function, $U(x_1, \ldots, x_n) = \min(x_1/a_1, \ldots, x_n/a_n)$.

The Cobb–Douglas case also requires some work. We will
show that as $\rho \to 0$, the ln of CES reduces to the ln of Cobb–
Douglas. The ln of CES, using the adding up of the α's to unity,
equals $\frac{\ln(\alpha_1 x_1^\rho + \cdots + \alpha_n x_n^\rho) - \ln(\alpha_1 x_1^0 + \cdots + \alpha_n x_n^0)}{\rho}$. For $\rho \to 0$, we get the
derivative of $\ln(\alpha_1 x_1^\rho + \cdots + \alpha_n x_n^\rho)$ in $\rho = 0$. By the chain rule
and the fact that $\frac{dx^\rho}{d\rho} = x^\rho \ln x$, we obtain $\frac{\alpha_1 x_1^\rho \ln x_1 + \cdots + \alpha_n x_n^\rho \ln x_n}{\alpha_1 x_1^\rho + \cdots + \alpha_n x_n^\rho}$
in $\rho = 0$, i.e. $\alpha_1 \ln x_1 + \cdots + \alpha_n \ln x_n$, which is the ln of Cobb–
Douglas indeed.

The vehicle for the measurement of price changes and
consumer's well-being is the expenditure function. We derive
it now. From equation (5.2), we see that, likewise,

$$x_i = x_1(\alpha_i/\alpha_1)^{1/(1-\rho)}(p_i/p_1)^{-1/(1-\rho)} \qquad (5.4)$$

Equation (5.4) shows that the quantity proportions are determined by the relative prices. The quantity level is determined by
the standard of living, u. To show this, substitute (5.4) into utility
(5.1). Then $u = x_1\left(\sum_{i=1}^{n}\alpha_i(\alpha_i/\alpha_1)^{\rho/(1-\rho)}(p_i/p_1)^{-\rho/(1-\rho)}\right)^{1/\rho} = x_1(\alpha_1/p_1)^{-1/(1-\rho)}\left(\sum_{i=1}^{n}\alpha_i^{1+\rho/(1-\rho)}p_i^{-\rho/(1-\rho)}\right)^{1/\rho}$. Solving for x_1

and substituting (5.3), we obtain

$$x_1 = (\alpha_1/p_1)^\sigma \left(\sum_{i=1}^{n} \alpha_i^\sigma p_i^{1-\sigma} \right)^{\sigma/(1-\sigma)} u.$$

Similarly, the demands for the other commodities, j, are

$$x_j = (\alpha_j/p_j)^\sigma \left(\sum_{i=1}^{n} \alpha_i^\sigma p_i^{1-\sigma} \right)^{\sigma/(1-\sigma)} u \tag{5.5}$$

Equation (5.5) shows demand for commodity j as a function of price and utility level, hence it is the jth component of compensated demand $x = D^c(p, u)$. Pricing these quantities by p_j and summing yields expenditure $(\sum_{i=1}^{n} \alpha_i^\sigma p_i^{1-\sigma})^{1+\sigma/(1-\sigma)} u$ or

$$e(p, u) = \left(\sum_{i=1}^{n} \alpha_i^\sigma p_i^{1-\sigma} \right)^{1/(1-\sigma)} u = I(p)u \tag{5.6}$$

The expenditure required to maintain a standard of living u is proportional to u. The coefficient is the *price index*,

$$I(p) = e(p, 1) = \left(\sum_{i=1}^{n} \alpha_i^\sigma p_i^{1-\sigma} \right)^{1/(1-\sigma)} \tag{5.7}$$

Equations (5.6) and (5.7) are a special case of price index equation (2.5) for homothetic utility functions. The presumption now is that utility is a CES function, see definition (5.1), with elasticity of substitution $\sigma = 1/(1 - \rho)$. Price index (5.7) is also a CES function, but a different one. The role of ρ in (5.1) is played by $1 - \sigma$ in (5.7). Consequently, the elasticity of substitution between the prices in the index is $1/(1 - (1 - \sigma)) = 1/\sigma$, which is the inverse of the elasticity of substitution between the quantities in the utility function. For example, if utility is Leontief, then, according to Table 5.1, the elasticity of substitution is zero. Hence, the price index has an infinite elasticity of substitution, implying it is linear, according to Table 5.1. By the same reasoning, the Cobb–Douglas function is reflexive: the price index is also Cobb–Douglas.

If prices are multiplied by a common factor, λ, then so is the price index, as follows:

$$I(\lambda p) = \lambda I(p) \tag{5.8}$$

If prices change from p to p', the expenditure required to maintain the standard of living increases by a factor $e(p', u)/e(p, u)$. The difference between this factor and one defines *inflation*, π. By equation (5.6), inflation amounts to

$$\pi = I(p')/I(p) - 1 \tag{5.9}$$

It is only a small step from compensated demand to ordinary demand. From equation (5.6), we obtain indirect utility

$$u = m \bigg/ \left(\sum_{i=1}^{n} \alpha_i^\sigma p_i^{1-\sigma} \right)^{1/(1-\sigma)} \tag{5.10}$$

and substitution of utility (5.10) in compensated demand (5.5) yields $x_j = m(\alpha_j/p_j)^\sigma \left(\sum_{i=1}^{n} \alpha_i^\sigma p_i^{1-\sigma} \right)^{\sigma/(1-\sigma)} \big/ \left(\sum_{i=1}^{n} \alpha_i^\sigma p_i^{1-\sigma} \right)^{1/(1-\sigma)}$. This simplifies to

$$x_i = D_i(p, m) = \frac{(\alpha_i/p_i)^\sigma m}{\alpha_1^\sigma p_1^{1-\sigma} + \cdots + \alpha_i^\sigma p_i^{1-\sigma} + \cdots + \alpha_n^\sigma p_n^{1-\sigma}} \tag{5.11}$$

We are now ready to find the measures of consumer's well-being discussed in the preceding chapters for CES functions. The measures are the equivalent variation, the compensating variation, and the consumer's surplus variation. First analyze the case where only prices change; income changes will be added later. The three measures are areas under demand functions between the old price vector p and the new price vector p'. Recall Figure 3.1; for the equivalent and compensating variations, the relevant demand functions are compensated demand functions and for the consumer's surplus variation the relevant demand function is the ordinary demand function.

In Chapter 3, we have seen that the equivalent variation is $E = \int_p^{p'} D^c\left(p'', u'\right) dp'' = \int_p^{p'} \frac{\partial e(p'', u')}{\partial p} dp'' = e(p', u') - e(p, u')$ (3.1). Substitution of result (5.6) yields that $E = [I(p') - I(p)]u'$. Usually prices tend to go up, and, therefore, since the budget set becomes smaller, utility goes down, $u' < u$. Likewise, the compensating variation is $C = [I(p') - I(p)]u$. The utility level, first u, then u', depends on the budget, $m = e(p, u) = e(p', u')$. In fact, by result (5.6), $m = I(p)u = I(p')u'$. Using this to eliminate u' and u from E and C, we obtain $E = m\{1 - [I(p')/I(p)]^{-1}\}$ and $C = m\{[I(p')/I(p)] - 1\}$. These measures are close. The first factors are equal. By equation (5.9), the second factors equal $1 - (1+\pi)^{-1}$ and π. However, because $(1+\pi)^{-1} = 1 - \pi + \pi^2 - \cdots$, the difference between the latter two factors is of the order π^2, which is small for a small rate of inflation π.

The compromise measure of the variation of consumer's surplus $S = \int_p^{p'} \left(D(p'', m)\, dp''\right.$ (4.2) was found only recently for CES functions, by ten Raa (2015a). First, we give the formula for the case of a price change in one commodity, i, that is for $S_i = \int_{p_i}^{p_i''} D_i \left(p_1, \ldots, p_{i-1}, p_i'', p_{i+1}, \ldots, p_{n,m}\right) dp_i''$.

Proposition 5.1. *CES variation of consumer's surplus is* $S_i = \frac{m}{1-\sigma} \ln\left\{1 + \left[\left(\frac{p_i'}{p_i}\right)^{1-\sigma} - 1\right] \frac{p_i x_i}{m}\right\}$, *where the quantities are given by* (5.11).

Before we prove Proposition 5.1, let us first check the sign of S when $p_i < p_i'$, to confirm it measures the *reduction* of consumer's surplus, as S was defined in (4.2). In other words, the expression better be positive. We distinguish two cases. If $\sigma < 1$, then $\left(\frac{p_i'}{p_i}\right)^{1-\sigma} > 1$, hence the ln in S_i is positive, hence S_i is positive. If $\sigma > 1$, then $\left(\frac{p_i'}{p_i}\right)^{1-\sigma} < 1$, hence the ln in S_i is negative, hence S_i is positive. If $\sigma \to 1$, then utility reduces to

$x_1^{\alpha_1} \ldots x_n^{\alpha_n}$, see Table 5.1. Hence, demand reduces to $x_i = \frac{\alpha_i m}{p_i}$ and, therefore, $S_i = \alpha_i m \ln \frac{p_i'}{p_i}$. Alternatively, one can show this is the limit of the expression in Proposition 5.1, using l'Hôpital's Rule. Anyway, S_i is also positive in this last case.

To prove Proposition 5.1, we must integrate CES demand (5.11) $\frac{(\alpha_i/p_i'')^\sigma m}{\alpha_1^\sigma p_1^{1-\sigma} + \cdots + \alpha_i^\sigma p_i''^{1-\sigma} + \cdots + \alpha_n^\sigma p_n^{1-\sigma}}$ with respect to p_i''. The primitive function is $\frac{m}{1-\sigma} \ln(\alpha_1^\sigma p_1^{1-\sigma} + \cdots + \alpha_i^\sigma p_i''^{1-\sigma} + \cdots + \alpha_n^\sigma p_n^{1-\sigma}) +$ constant. For the constant, choose $\frac{m}{1-\sigma} \ln\left(\frac{p_i^\sigma x_i}{\alpha_i^\sigma}\right)$. Then the primitive function becomes $\frac{m}{1-\sigma} \ln\left[\left(\frac{\alpha_1}{\alpha_i}\right)^\sigma \left(\frac{p_1}{p_i}\right)^{-\sigma} p_1 x_i + \cdots + \left(\frac{p_i''}{p_i}\right)^{-\sigma} p_i'' x_i + \cdots + \left(\frac{\alpha_n}{\alpha_i}\right)^\sigma \left(\frac{p_n}{p_i}\right)^{-\sigma}\right]$ However, since demand is generated by budget constrained utility maximization, the ratio of the marginal utilities equals the price ratio, $\frac{\alpha_1}{\alpha_i}\left(\frac{x_1}{x_i}\right)^{\rho-1} = \frac{p_1}{p_i}$, or, invoking (5.3), $\left(\frac{\alpha_1}{\alpha_i}\right)^\sigma \left(\frac{p_1}{p_i}\right)^{-\sigma} = \frac{x_1}{x_i}$ and likewise for all terms except the ith one. Thus, the terms under the ln in the primitive function reduce to $p_1 x_1 + \cdots + p_i''^{1-\sigma} p_i^\sigma x_i + \cdots + p_n x_n = m + (p_i''^{1-\sigma} p_i^\sigma - p_i) x_i$. Premultiplying by $\frac{m}{1-\sigma}$, evaluating in $p_i'' = p_i'$ and $p_i'' = p_i$, and subtracting, the variation of consumer's surplus becomes $\frac{m}{1-\sigma} \ln \frac{m + (p_i'^{1-\sigma} p_i^\sigma - p_i) x_i}{m} = \frac{m}{1-\sigma} \ln\left\{1 + \left[\left(\frac{p_i'}{p_i}\right)^{1-\sigma} - 1\right] \frac{p_i x_i}{m}\right\}$. This completes the proof of Proposition 5.1. $\qquad\square$

Proposition 5.1 is discussed now. First of all, consumer's surplus (4.1) with subscript i — as we focus on a price change of that commodity — is obtained by letting $p_i' \to \infty$ and converges if the elasticity of substitution exceeds that of the Cobb–Douglas function, i.e. when $\sigma > 1$. Then the term in Proposition 5.1 featuring p_i' vanishes and, using definition (4.2), $CS_i = CS_i - 0 = S_i = \frac{m}{1-\sigma} \ln \frac{m - p_i x_i}{m}$. If the expenditure on commodity i is a small fraction of income, then this may be approximated by $\frac{m}{1-\sigma} \frac{-p_i x_i}{m} = \frac{p_i x_i}{\sigma-1}$. The importance of a commodity, in terms of consumer's surplus, is proportional to the expenditure on it, but inversely proportional to the elasticity of substitution. If there are good substitutes, a price increase has little impact.

The extension to the case of several, simultaneous price changes, is as follows. The variation of consumer's surplus, (4.2), is a line integral of demand, from vector p to vector p'. At least in principle, the value of the line integral may depend on the path taken from p to p'. However, that is not the case for CES utility, as will be argued now. From the proof of Proposition 5.1, we know that the primitive of demand function (5.11) with respect to price is $\frac{m}{1-\sigma} \ln(\alpha_1^\sigma p_1^{1-\sigma} + \cdots + \alpha_i^\sigma p_i^{1-\sigma} + \cdots + \alpha_n^\sigma p_n^{1-\sigma})$. But this primitive is equal to $m \ln I(p)$, by definition (5.7) of the price index I. In short, for CES demand we have

$$\int D(p,m)dp = m \ln I(p) \tag{5.12}$$

This line integral value depends only on the values of the price index in the end point and in the start point of the path of integration. Hence, the variation of consumer's surplus (4.2) equals $m \ln[I(p')/I(p)]$. This path independence result of the variation consumer's surplus holds for homothetic demands, see Proposition 4.1.

A widely used variant of CES function (5.1) is the CES function with *residual demand*. The idea is that the commodities $x_1, \ldots, x_n$ are the focus of the analyst and that the consumer need not spend the entire budget but uses the residual income for all other things. The residual demand is aggregated in scalar x_0. The utility function is

$$U(x_0, x_1, \ldots, x_n) = x_0 + (\alpha_1 x_1^\rho + \cdots + \alpha_n x_n^\rho)^{r/\rho} \tag{5.13}$$

If in (5.13) parameter $r = 1$, utility is homothetic and demand will be concentrated in either the differentiated commodities or the residual commodity, depending on the price index (5.7) relative to the price of the residual commodity, which is usually set one, as can be done by rescaling the numeraire residual demand. Anyway, this brings us back to the CES function without residual demand. Likewise, we get uninteresting corner solutions with residual demand zero, exhausting the budget if $r > 1$. Hence, we assume $0 < r < 1$ in (5.13).

The available budget, say $\underline{m}$, is now divided between expenditure m on the differentiated commodities and expenditure $\underline{m} - m$ on residual demand x_0, of which the price is one. The demands for the differentiated commodities are given by equation (5.11). The expenditure on the differentiated commodities or, equivalently, the residual demand, is determined by the condition that the marginal utility of the bundle of differentiated commodities with respect to expenditure equals one. Since the variant utility (5.13) involves power r, using equation (5.10), the differentiated commodities contribute utility $u = \left(\sum_{i=1}^{n} \alpha_i^\sigma p_i^{1-\sigma} \right)^{r/(\sigma-1)} m^r$. Differentiating with respect to m the optimality condition reads $r \left(\sum_{i=1}^{n} \alpha_i^\sigma p_i^{1-\sigma} \right)^{r/(\sigma-1)} m^{r-1} = 1$.

Solving, the optimal expenditure on the differentiated commodities will be $m(p) = r^{r/(1-r)} \left(\sum_{i=1}^{n} \alpha_i^\sigma p_i^{1-\sigma} \right)^{\frac{1}{(1/r-1)(\sigma-1)}}$. Substituting back, demand (5.11) becomes

$$D_i(p, m) = r^{1/(1-r)} (\alpha_i/p_i)^\sigma (\alpha_1^\sigma p_1^{1-\sigma} + \cdots + \alpha_n^\sigma p_n^{1-\sigma})^{\frac{1/(1-r)-\sigma}{\sigma-1}}$$

$$(5.14)$$

Proposition 5.2. *With residual demand CES consumer's surplus equals* $(1/r - 1) r^{1/(1-r)} (\alpha_1^\sigma p_1^{1-\sigma} + \cdots + \alpha_n^\sigma p_n^{1-\sigma})^{\frac{1}{(1/r-1)(\sigma-1)}}$.

Proof. We must integrate, see CES demand (5.14), $(\alpha_1^\sigma p_1^{1-\sigma} + \cdots + \alpha_i^\sigma p_i'^{1-\sigma} + \cdots + \alpha_n^\sigma p_n^{1-\sigma})^{\frac{1/(1-r)-\sigma}{\sigma-1}} (\alpha_i/p_i')^\sigma$ with respect to p_i' from p_i to infinity. The primitive function is $\frac{1}{1-\sigma} \frac{1/r-1}{1/\rho-1} (\alpha_1^\sigma p_1^{1-\sigma} + \cdots + \alpha_i^\sigma p_i'^{1-\sigma} + \cdots + \alpha_n^\sigma p_n^{1-\sigma})^{\frac{1}{(1/r-1)(\sigma-1)}} = (1 - 1/r)(\alpha_1^\sigma p_1^{1-\sigma} + \cdots + \alpha_i^\sigma p_i'^{1-\sigma} + \cdots + \alpha_n^\sigma p_n^{1-\sigma})^{\frac{1}{(1/r-1)(\sigma-1)}}$. Since this behaves like $p_i'^{(1-\sigma)\frac{1/\rho-1}{1/r-1}} = p_i'^{\frac{1}{1-1/r}}$, using (5.3), which tends to zero by assumption $r < 1$, the upper bound is zero. Hence, invoking a negative sign for the lower bound and picking up demand factor $r^{1/(1-r)}$ from (5.14), consumer's surplus is as posted.   □

In the *symmetric* case, $\alpha_i = \alpha$ and $p_i = p$, Proposition 5.2 becomes as follows. Demand reduces to $D_i(p,m) = r^{1/(1-r)}(\alpha/p)^\sigma(n\alpha^\sigma p^{1-\sigma})^{\frac{1/(1-r)-\sigma}{\sigma-1}}$. The price elasticity, i.e. the power of p, reduces to $-1/(1-r)$, which is independent of the elasticity of substitution. However, the elasticity of substitution does impact the level of demand, through the power of α, which features $\rho{:}\sigma\left(1 + \frac{1/(1-r)-\sigma}{\sigma-1}\right) = \frac{\sigma}{\sigma-1}\left(-1 + \frac{1}{1-r}\right) = \frac{1/\rho}{1/r-1}$. Complementarity (as measured by a lower value of ρ or, equivalently, of σ) boosts demand and hence consumer's surplus (for $\alpha > 1$, as will be the case). Consumer's surplus in the symmetric case reduces to

$$(1/r - 1)r^{1/(1-r)}n^{\frac{1}{(1/r-1)(\sigma-1)}}\alpha^{\frac{\sigma}{(1/r-1)(\sigma-1)}}/p^{\frac{1}{1/r-1}} \qquad (5.15)$$

In his work, ten Raa (2015a) uses CES consumer's surplus formula (5.15) to determine and compare the monopoly and optimum provisions of variety. The analysis is in the tradition of Dixit and Stiglitz (1977, p. 301), who 'have a rather surprising case where the monopolistic competition equilibrium is identical with the optimum constrained by the lack of lump sum subsidies.' In their case, utility is a function of the numeraire and the symmetric CES aggregate $(x_1^\rho + \cdots + x_n^\rho)^{1/\rho}$. The number of varieties, n, is determined by market forces or a nonnegative profit constrained welfare optimization. Consumers have taste for variety. The utility gain derived from spreading a unit of production between n differentiated products is $[(1/n)^\rho + \cdots + (1/n)^\rho]^{1/\rho}/1 = [n(1/n)^\rho]^{1/\rho} = n^{(1-\rho)/\rho}$. Benassy (1996) defines the elasticity of the taste variety in the obvious way and thus shows it equals to $1/\rho - 1$ in the Dixit–Stiglitz framework. The elasticity of demand is $\sigma = 1/(1-\rho)$ and monopolistic profit maximization yields that the markup relative to price is the inverse elasticity $(p-c)/p = 1/\sigma$ or that the markup relative to cost c is $(p - c)/p = p/c - 1 = (1 - 1/\sigma)^{-1} - 1 = [1 - (1 - \rho)]^{-1} - 1 = 1/\rho - 1$. Benassy (1996) shows that this coincidence of taste for variety and markup explains the Dixit–Stiglitz result and introduces a multiplicative power function of n in the CES aggregate to control for the variety elasticity independent of the demand elasticity or markup.

In the symmetric Dixit–Stiglitz model, consumers maximize $U(\underline{m} - npx, (x^\rho + \cdots + x^\rho)^{1/\rho}) = U(\underline{m} - npx, n^{1/\rho}x)$. ten Raa (2015a) uses the following instance of (5.13) as utility: $U(x_0, x_1, \ldots, x_n) = x_0 + n^{\nu + r - r/\rho}(x_1^\rho + \cdots + x_n^\rho)^{r/\rho}$. The multiplicative coefficient has been chosen following Benassy (1996); ν is the variety elasticity. Indeed, in the symmetric case the second utility term is $n^{\nu + r - r/\rho}[(m/np)^\rho + \cdots + (m/np)^\rho]^{r/\rho} = n^{\nu + r - r/\rho}[n(m/np)^\rho]^{r/\rho} = n^\nu (m/p)^r$. The connection with (5.13) is $(\alpha_1 x_1^\rho + \cdots + \alpha_n x_n^\rho)^{r/\rho} = n^{\nu + r - r/\rho}(x_1^\rho + \cdots + x_n^\rho)^{r/\rho} = (n^{\nu\rho/r + \rho - 1}x_1^\rho + \cdots + n^{\nu\rho/r + \rho - 1}x_n^\rho)^{r/\rho}$ or

$$\alpha_1 = \cdots = \alpha_n = \alpha = n^{\nu\rho/r + \rho - 1} \tag{5.16}$$

The budget constraint of the consumer is binding and can be used to eliminate residual income x_0. Then the constant income term m may be deleted, and, in the symmetric case, utility reduces to $n^{\nu + r - r/\rho}(nx^\rho)^{r/\rho} - npx$. In short, *utility* is $n^{\nu + r}x^r - npx$. Demand is determined by setting the derivative of utility equal to zero. Multiplying through by x,

$$npx = n^{\nu + r}rx^r \tag{5.17}$$

The left-hand side of (5.17) is *revenue*. The implicit assumption is that income is greater than this expression, ruling out the corner solution where all income is spent on the differentiated commodities offered by the monopolist. (Since we will solve for quantities and variety, the lower bound of income is a function of the parameters.) Dividing (5.17) by np and rewriting, we see that *demand* is $x = (n^{\nu + r - 1}r/p)^{1/(1-r)}$. For each variety, let the set-up cost be F and the marginal cost be c. Then *profit* — revenue (5.15) minus cost — is

$$n^{\nu+r}rx^r - cnx - nF \qquad (5.18)$$

We will determine and compare the monopoly variety, the second-best variety and the first-best variety. The *monopoly variety* is determined as follows. Maximizing (5.18), the first-order condition with respect to x yields

$$x = (n^{\nu+r-1}r^2/c)^{1/(1-r)} \qquad (5.19)$$

And the first-order condition with respect to n is

$$(\nu + r)n^{\nu+r-1}rx^r - cx - F \qquad (5.20)$$

Following Dixit and Stiglitz (1977), Anderson *et al.* (1992), and Benassy (1996), equation (5.19) ignores the integer problem.

We assume that there is taste for variety, but with diminishing returns: the elasticity fulfills the following maintained

Assumption: The variety elasticity, ν, is less than $1 - r$, where r is the utility elasticity of the differentiated products.

This assumption ensures the first-order conditions solve, barring bang-bang behavior. In fact, the *monopoly variety* is

$$n = \left(\frac{\nu^{1-r}r^{1+r}}{F^{1-r}c^r}\right)^{\frac{1}{1-r-\nu}} \qquad (5.21)$$

Proof: Substitute (5.19) into (5.20): $(\nu + r)n^{\nu+r-1}r(n^{\nu+r-1}r^2/c)^{r/(1-r)} - c(n^{\nu+r-1}r^2/c)^{1/(1-r)} - F = 0$. In the first and the second terms, the powers of $1/c$ sum to a common $r/(1-r)$ and the powers of n sum to a common $(\nu + r - 1)/(1 - r)$. Hence, consolidating the first two terms, the equation becomes $[(\nu+r)r(r^2)^{r/(1-r)} - (r^2)^{1/(1-r)}](1/c)^{r/(1-r)}n^{(\nu+r-1)/(1-r)} = F$. In the bracketed expression, the middle term equals $(r^2)^{1+r/(1-r)}$ and cancels against the third term. Hence, the bracketed expression reduces to $[\nu r(r^2)^{r/(1-r)}] = \nu r^{(1+r)/(1-r)}$ and the equation becomes $\nu r^{(1+r)/(1-r)}(1/c)^{r/(1-r)}n^{(\nu+r-1)/(1-r)} = F$ or $\nu^{1-r}r^{1+r}c^{-r}n^{\nu+r-1} = F^{1-r}$ or $n^{1-r-\nu} = \frac{\nu^{1-r}r^{1+r}}{F^{1-r}c^r}$, from which (5.21) follows. ☐

The *second-best variety* maximizes surplus but subject to the constraint that profit is nonnegative. As we will confirm later, in the first best solution price equals marginal cost, hence profit is negative. In the second-best solution, profit must be nonnegative and this constraint is binding. The second-best variety is

$$n = \left(\frac{\nu^{1-r}r^r}{F^{1-r}c^r(1+\nu/r)}\right)^{\frac{1}{1-r-\nu}} \tag{5.22}$$

Proof: We will use the first-order condition of constrained maximization that the objective function (consumer's surplus) and the constraint function (profit) must have equal marginal rates of substitution. The profit function $n^{\nu+r}rx^r - cnx - nF$ (5.19) has marginal rate of substitution (between variety n and quantity x) $\frac{(\nu+r)n^{\nu+r-1}rx^r-cx-F}{n^{\nu+r}r^2x^{r-1}-cn}$ or, substituting the zero-profit condition, $\frac{(\nu+r-1)n^{\nu+r-1}rx^r}{n^{\nu+r}r^2x^{r-1}-cn}$. Turn to consumer's surplus (5.15). By equations (5.16) and (5.3), $\alpha^\sigma = n^{\nu\rho\sigma/r+\rho\sigma-\sigma} = n^{\nu(\sigma-1)/r-1}$. Hence, the powers of n and of α in (5.15) can be consolidated into a single power of n, with exponent $\frac{1+\nu(\sigma-1)/r-1}{(1/r-1)(\sigma-1)} = \frac{\nu}{1-r}$, so that consumer's surplus becomes $(1/r - 1)r^{1/(1-r)}n^{\frac{\nu}{1-r}}/p^{\frac{1}{1/r-1}}$. Substituting inverse demand, which is readily available from (5.17), and simplifying, consumer's surplus can be rewritten as $(1/r-1)r^{1/(1-r)}n^{\nu/(1-r)}/(n^{\nu+r-1}rx^{r-1})^{\frac{1}{1/r-1}} = (1-r)n^{\nu+r}x^r$. It implies a marginal rate of substitution (between n and x) of $\frac{(\nu+r)/n}{r/x} = (1+\nu/r)x/n$. The first-order condition of the maximization of consumer's surplus subject to the producer surplus constraint is that the marginal rates of substitution of producer and consumer's surplus are equal. Solving, $x^{1-r} = \frac{n^{\nu+r-1}r}{(1+\nu/r)c}$. By (5.17), $p = n^{\nu+r-1}rx^{r-1} = n^{\nu+r-1}r\frac{(1+\nu/r)c}{n^{\nu+r-1}r} = (1+\nu/r)c$. By the zero-profit condition the markup offsets the fixed cost: $(\nu/r)cx = F$. Hence, $x = rF/\nu c$, which is independent of n. Combining the last two expressions for x, $(rF/\nu c)^{1-r} = \frac{n^{\nu+r-1}r}{(1+\nu/r)c}$. Solving for n yields (5.22). $\qquad\square$

The *first-best variety* maximizes total surplus, the sum of consumer's and producer's surplus,

$$n = \left(\frac{\nu^{1-r}r^r}{F^{1-r}c^r} \right)^{\frac{1}{1-r-\nu}} \qquad (5.23)$$

Proof: The derivative of consumer's surplus with respect to p_i is minus the demand for that commodity, $-D_i$. The derivative of producer's surplus $(p_1 - c)D_1 + \cdots + (p_n - c)D_n - nF$ with respect to p_i is $D_i + (p_1 - c)\partial D_1/\partial p_i + \cdots + (p_n - c)D_n/\partial p_i$. Setting the sum of the derivatives equal to zero, the first-order condition of total surplus maximization with respect to price reads $(p_1 - c)\partial D_1/\partial p_i + \cdots + (p_n - c)D_n/\partial p_i = 0$, $i = 1, \ldots, n$. By symmetry and homogeneity of the differentiated commodities demand (of degree $1/(r-1) < 0$), we conclude the familiar first best condition $p_i = c$. From the proof of (5.22) we know that consumer's surplus is equal to $(1/r-1)r^{1/(1-r)}n^{\frac{\nu}{1-r}}/p^{\frac{1}{1/r-1}}$. It follows that the sum of consumer's plus producer's surplus is $(1/r - 1)r^{1/(1-r)}n^{\frac{\nu}{1-r}}/p^{\frac{1}{1/r-1}} - nF$. The first-order condition for total surplus maximization is $(1/r - 1)r^{1/(1-r)}\frac{\nu}{1-r}n^{\frac{\nu}{1-r}-1}c^{\frac{-1}{1/r-1}} = F$. Solving for n yields (5.23). $\qquad\square$

We now compare the monopoly, second-best, and first-best variety solutions. We use the assumption that the variety elasticity, ν, is less than $1 - r$, where r is the utility elasticity of the differentiated products. The ratio of the monopoly variety (5.21) to the second-best variety (5.22) is $(r + \nu)^{\frac{1}{1-r-\nu}} < 1$ because $r + \nu < 1$ and, therefore, the exponent is positive. A *monopolist underprovides variety relative to the second-best variety*. The ratio of the second-best (5.22) to the first-best (5.23) variety is $1/(1+\nu/r)^{\frac{1}{1-r-\nu}} < 1$ because the exponent is positive.

Second-best variety is less than first-best variety. This welfare analysis of variety illustrates the use of the novel CES consumer's surplus formulas.

This chapter has provided the formulas of CES consumer's surplus. It remains to be seen if the concept is theoretically sound. Does it measure consumer's well-being? Unfortunately, it does not really, as the next chapter will analyze in detail. Chapter 6 will discuss the issue in a concrete way, revealing shortcomings in a suggestive way, enabling us to modify the concept of consumer's surplus in Chapters 8 and 9.

Chapter 6

Utility Tracking Measures of Well-being

In this chapter, we will analyze the three main measures of consumer's well-being — the equivalent and compensating variations and consumer's surplus — in terms of their capabilities to track utility. A good well-being measure moves in the same direction as utility: when utility goes up (or down), a well-being measure ought to go up (or down) as well. Unfortunately, we will see that all three measures fail the test, hence do not track utility. However, when income is constant, we will see some positive result. Moreover, when income changes, we will be able to disentangle the price and income effects on utility. This will be shown explicitly for CES utility functions in this chapter and the analysis will be generalized to homothetic and even some nonhomothetic utility functions in Chapters 8 and 9.

CES demands have a nice property, namely a tight relationship between consumer's surplus and utility. In the first part of the analysis, the budget is assumed constant. Proposition 6.1 shows the variation of CES consumer's surplus is proportional to the logarithmic change in utility, which is independent of income, and that the proportionality coefficient equals income. This rich structure will facilitate analysis of the situation when income changes along with the change in price.

Proposition 6.1. *The variation of CES consumer's surplus equals* $S = m \ln[V(p, m)/V(p', m)] = m \ln[V(p, 1)/\ln V(p', 1)]$, *i.e. the product of the budget,* m, *and the logarithmic change in utility,* $\ln V(p, m) - \ln V(p', m)$.

Proof. By equations (4.2) and (5.12), $S = CS(p, m) - CS(p', m) = \int_p^{p'} D(p'', m)dp'' = m \ln[I(p')/I(p)]$. Substituting equation (5.6), i.e. $m = e(p, u) = I(p)u = I(p)V(p, m)$, yields the first equality, $S = m \ln[V(p, m)/V(p', m)]$. Indirect utility expression (5.10) yields the second equality. □

Proposition 6.1 is in terms of the *variation* of consumer's surplus. Consumer's surplus itself, $CS(p, m) = \int_p^{\infty} D(p', m)dp'$ (4.1), is problematic because it diverges. To show this, note that the latter expression equals the variation of consumer's surplus between p and $p' = \infty$, i.e. using Proposition 6.1, $m \ln V(p, m) - m \ln V(\infty, m)$. However, $V(\infty, m) = U(0) = 0$ and $\ln 0$ is $-\infty$, hence $CS(p, m) = \infty$. The taking of the variation of consumer's surplus in Proposition 6.1 circumvents this issue.

The variation of consumer's surplus relative to a base year is a natural candidate well-being measure. Normally, prices in the base year are equal to one, but to simplify the mathematics we pick base year prices equal to the CES parameters, $\alpha_1, \ldots, \alpha_n$, respectively. Thus, instead of a price change from p to p', consider a price change from vector α to p. Proposition 6.1's variation of consumer's surplus becomes $S = m \ln[V(\alpha, m)/V(p, m)]$. If p is greater than α, indirect utility $V(p, m)$ will be smaller than $V(\alpha, m)$, and, therefore, S will be positive. Indeed, the variation of consumer's surplus was defined as the reduction of consumer's surplus. The consumer's surplus *gain* is the opposite: $S = -m \ln[V(\alpha, m)/V(p, m)] = m \ln[V(p, m)/V(\alpha, m)]$. Now by (5.6), (5.7) and the fact that the CES coefficients α_i may be assumed to sum to unity, $V(\alpha, m) = m/I(\alpha) = m$. Hence, the consumer's surplus gain reduces to

$$S = m \ln V(p, m) - m \ln m \tag{6.1}$$

Equation (6.1) shows that if m is constant, the CES-based consumer's surplus gain tracks utility, as it is an increasing function of $V(p, m)$ (see the concept in Chapter 1). This confirms Proposition 4.1, by which the variation of consumer's surplus measures welfare, provided utility is homothetic and income is constant.

Now let us address the important issue of welfare measurement when both price and income vary. Then there is a problem, even when utility is homothetic, as will be discussed now. It is natural to continue considering consumer's surplus gain (6.1) as a well-being measure, or, rewriting the right-hand side: $W(p, m) = m \ln[V(p, m)/m]$. While we have just seen that this measure tracks utility if income m is constant, we will see next that it no longer does so when income varies. We employ Proposition 1.1, according to which a utility tracking well-being measure must pass the homogeneity test (1.1), i.e. be homogeneous of degree zero in prices and the budget. To check if this condition holds, we must consider proportionate changes of the prices and the budget: from p to sp and from m to sm. Using the homogeneity of degree zero of indirect utility (see Chapter 1), $W(sp, sm) = sm \ln[V(sp, sm)/(sm)] = sm \ln[V(p, m)/(sm)] = sW(p, m) - sm \ln s$. This equals $W(p, m)$ indeed if $s = 1$. The equality $W(sp, sm) = W(p, m)$ holds around $s = 1$ only if the derivatives of $sW(p, m) - sm \ln s$ with respect to s are zero in $s = 1$. That is, $W(p, m) - m \ln s - sm/s = 0$ (first derivative) and $-m/s = 0$ or $m = 0$ (second derivative). Hence, consumer's surplus gain fails the homogeneity test (1.1) for nonzero m. By Proposition 1.1, *the consumer's surplus gain does not track utility when both price and income vary.*

A 'fix' in the literature runs as follows. I write 'fix' in quotes because the result will prove of limited value. However, let me first present the procedure. The construct departs from $D(p,m)dp+dm = du/\lambda$ (4.5) and integrates this expression from (p,m) to (p',m'). As we have seen in Chapter 4, the value of the line integral depends on the path of integration in the price–income space. This pain can be turned a pleasure by showing that there exists a path for which the value tracks utility (Stahl, 1983; ten Raa, 2013, Section 5.6). Recall from Table 4.1 that the combined well-being impacts of a price increase and a budget change are approximated by the following monetary measure:

$$\Delta \text{budget} - S = m' - m - [CS(p,m) - CS(p',m')]$$
$$= CS(p',m') - CS(p,m) + m' - m \quad (6.2)$$

Because price features in the lower bound of CS integral (4.1), the first two terms result from integrating $-D(p,m)dp$ in (4.5), and the second result trivially from integrating dm. Now chose the following path of integration. First, change income from m to some intermediate m'', then change price from p to p', and finally change income from m'' to m'. This yields the following expression: $CS(p',m'') - CS(p,m'') + m' - m$. This measure, due to ten Raa (2013, p. 96), depends on the choice of intermediate value, m''. The path of integration is a zigzag, first in the direction of income, then of price, and finally of income again. The value of the monetary measure depends on the location of the crossover. By equation (5.12), the monetary measure amounts to $-\int D(p,m)dp + m' - m = -m'' \ln I(p') + m'' \ln I(p) + m' - m$. By equation (5.6), $I(p') = m'/u'$ and $I(p) = m/u$. Hence, the monetary measure becomes $-m''(\ln m' - \ln u') + m''(\ln m - \ln u) + m' - m = m'' \ln u' - m'' \ln u + m' - m - m''(\ln m' - \ln m)$. This measure tracks utility if it is positive for $u' > u$ and negative for $u' < u$. Now choose $m'' = (m' - m)/(\ln m' - \ln m)$. Then the last four terms in the monetary measure, $m' - m - m''(\ln m' - \ln m)$, cancel and, therefore, only the first two remain, i.e. $m'' \ln(u'/u)$. So, for this value of m'' the measure tracks utility.

As a technical note we show that the chosen m'' is an intermediate value of m and m'. First, if $m' > m$, we must show $m \leq (m' - m)/(\ln m' - \ln m) \leq m'$. Dividing by m and defining $x = m'/m$, we must show $1 \leq (x - 1)/\ln x \leq x$, or, inverting, $1/x \leq \ln x/(x - 1) \leq 1$, or, multiplying by $x - 1 > 0$, $(x-1)/x \leq \ln x \leq x-1$. The right-hand inequality $\ln x \leq x-1$ is a known validity for $x > 0$ and if we apply it to $1/x$, we obtain $-\ln x \leq 1/x - 1$, i.e. the left-hand inequality. Second, if $m' < m$, we must show $m' \leq (m' - m)/(\ln m' - \ln m) \leq m$ or $m' \leq (m - m')/(\ln m - \ln m') \leq m$, but this is the same as the first case, with the roles of m and m' reversed.

We conclude that there exists an integration path for the consumer's surplus measure, or, equivalently, an intermediate income level at which consumer's surplus can be measured, such that the measure tracks utility. However, this result is of limited value for two reasons. First, it is not practical. The information needed is so large that one could just as well determine indirect utility itself. This point has been made by Hausman (1981). Second, it masks the fundamental shortcoming of consumer's surplus that it is not homogeneous of degree zero. The underlying problem is that consumer's surplus is a monetary measure. From Figure 4.1 we know that consumer's surplus is the area between the demand curve, which indicates the consumer's willingness to pay, and the price line. The area can be found by calculating this difference for every unit sold and summing over the units sold. The magnitude of this measure depends on the monetary unit. If we use euro's instead of Irish pounds (remember 1 Irish pound was replaced by 1.27 euros), consumer's surplus increases by 27%. The same holds for the other component of the well-being measure, the change in income, $m' - m$.

Another fix of the incapacity of consumer's surplus to track utility when price and income change one may try is to replace consumer's surplus by one of the so-called exact measures, equivalent variation or compensating variation. The main drawback of this fix is that it relies on unobserved concepts, although Hausman (1981) has argued that in principle they can be estimated given sufficiently many demand data.

Consider the *equivalent variation*, in case of a price change from p to p'. The equivalent variation is $E = m - e(p, u')$. If p' is greater than p, utility u' will be smaller than u, and, therefore, E will be positive. Indeed, the equivalent variation was defined as a measure of the loss of welfare. The gain of welfare is measured by the opposite, that is $-E = e(p, u') - m$. As in the case of consumer's surplus (6.1), if m is constant, this measure tracks utility. However, also as in the case of consumer's surplus, it no longer does so when income varies, from m to m'. The situation is again path dependent, and a suitable path can be chosen. Recall from Table 4.1 that the combined well-being impacts of a price increase and a budget change are approximated by the monetary measure Δbudget $- E$. The path is rectangular, as follows. First, change income from m to m' and then change price from p to p', evaluating $-E$ at income m'. The monetary measure becomes $m' - m + e(p, u') - m' = e(p, u') - e(p, u)$, the change in equivalent variation at price p. This monetary measure tracks utility, but it is tricky, because the equivalent variation component, $e(p, u') - m' = e(p, u') - e(p', u')$, measures the price effect at the new income level, unlike the equivalent variation-based measure in Table 4.1.

Similarly, one may base a monetary measure on the *compensating variation*, $C = e(p', u) - m$. The gain of welfare is measured by the opposite, $-C = m - e(p', u)$. Recall from Table 4.1 that the combined well-being impacts of a price increase and a budget change are approximated by the monetary measure Δbudget $- C$. The path is a rectangular one, again, but now as follows. First, change income, from p to p', and then change price, from m to m'. The monetary measure becomes $m' - m + m - e(p', u) = e(p', u') - e(p', u)$, the change in equivalent variation at price p'. This monetary measure tracks utility as well.

The commonality of the equivalent and compensating variation-based monetary measures is that they are changes in expenditure function values at given prices (p and p', respectively). Indeed, the expenditure function is increasing in utility, hence there is a monotonic transformation of utility to money at fixed prices.

Let us recall how different monetary measures of consumer's well-being track utility. In Chapter 4, we analyzed a consumer with a symmetric Cobb–Douglas utility function who was impacted by a price increase and a budget increase. For the budget increase, we considered three alternative values. Table 4.1 contrasted the change in utility with three monetary measures, namely the budget increase minus equivalent variation, the budget increase minus consumer surplus variation, and the budget increase minus compensating variation. The first measure overestimated the change in utility thrice, even overestimated in terms of sign. The second measure overestimated the change in utility twice, in terms of sign. The last measure correctly estimated the change in utility, in terms of sign, but by swapping the initial and end situations, the third measure was shown to have the same flaw as the first measure. Summarizing, all three measures fail as a welfare measure. The problem is that none of the measures passes the homogeneity test (1.1) (see Proposition 1.1). The monetary dimension of the measures is the cause of their failures.

The key to finding a utility tracking measure is suggested by Proposition 6.1's result, that the variation of CES consumer's surplus is the product of the budget and the logarithm of relative utility, $S = m \ln V(p, m) - m \ln V(p', m)$. Here, V is the indirect CES utility function, given by equation (5.10). Proposition 6.1 implies

$$S/m = \ln V(p, m) - \ln V(p', m) \qquad (6.3)$$

The left-hand side of equation (6.3) is a dimensionless variant of consumer's surplus, while the right-hand side tracks utility if only price changes. This variant of consumer's surplus is a key element of the consumer's index that will be developed in Chapters 8 and 9. It must be augmented by a term representing the change in budget. That income term must also be dimensionless. The conventional monetary measures are $(m' - m) - S$, as well as $(m' - m) - E$ and $(m' - m) - C$. Failing homogeneity test (1.1), these three measures do not track utility. In each case, the budget term is $m' - m$, which is not dimensionless. Instead, we will employ $\ln m' - \ln m$, which is a dimensionless growth rate. These two modifications of consumer's surplus, the normalizations of consumer's surplus variation and of the budget, will do the trick and provide us with a measure of consumer well-being that tracks utility, not only for CES functions, but for all homothetic and even some nonhomothetic utility functions. The analysis will be done in Chapters 7, 8, and 9.

Chapter 7

Price Indices

Price indices are used to measure changes in the cost of living and the standard of living. Before we present price index formulas, let us first discuss the concepts. The organizing principle is that of the expenditure function, $m = e(p, u)$, which for any price vector p maps ordinal utility u to cardinal money m, a practical transformation. Consider a price vector change from p to p' and a simultaneous income change from m to m'. Utility becomes u'. The Hicksian measures are the equivalent variation, $E = e(p', u') - e(p, u')$, and the compensating variation $C = e(p', u) - e(p, u)$; see equations (3.1) and (3.2). In Chapter 3, we derived standard of living measures and made them invariant with respect to the monetary unit by taking the logarithms of expenditure or, equivalently, taking the ratio of the expenditures, instead of the differences. The same procedure works here. The equivalent variation-based cost-of-living index is $e(p', u')/e(p, u')$ and, likewise, the compensating variation-based cost-of-living index is $e(p', u)/e(p, u)$. The first ratio is Jorgenson's (1990) measure of the cost of living; hence his measure is equivalent variation-based, as is his measure of the standard of living (see Chapter 3). These cost-of-living indices depend on the expenditure function, which in turn depends on the underlying utility functions. For small changes, however, this dependence dissolves, and we have more generally applicable price indices.

A price index is a weighted average of prices, $p_1, \ldots, p_n$, where n is the number of goods and services, and the rate of change of a price index is a measure of inflation. Natural weights are the budget shares, $p_i x_i / px$, $i = 1, \ldots, n$. This choice of weights defines the *Divisia index* of inflation,

$$\sum_{i=1}^{n} \frac{p_i x_i}{px} \frac{dp_i}{p_i} \qquad (7.1)$$

The Divisia (1925) index has the nice property that it measures the rate of income change required to maintain the standard of living. This property will be demonstrated on the presumption of local nonsatiation.

The consumer attains utility $U(D(p, m))$. To maintain this standard of living when price changes by dp, income must change by dm such that $du = \frac{\partial U}{\partial x}\left(\frac{\partial D}{\partial p}dp + \frac{\partial D}{\partial m}dm\right) = 0$. Now the first-order condition of the problem of the consumer, (2.1), is $p = \lambda \frac{\partial U}{\partial x}$, where λ is the Lagrange multiplier. Hence, $\lambda du = p\left(\frac{\partial D}{\partial p}dp + \frac{\partial D}{\partial m}dm\right) = 0$. Assuming local nonsatiation, Slutsky equation (Chapter 2) yields, substituting equation (2.6), $p\frac{\partial D}{\partial p} = 0^{\mathrm{T}} - p\frac{\partial D}{\partial m}D^{\mathrm{T}}$. Combining the last two equations, $p\frac{\partial D}{\partial m}dm = p\frac{\partial D}{\partial m}D^{\mathrm{T}}dp$. Dividing through by scalar $p\frac{\partial D}{\partial m}$, $dm = D^{\mathrm{T}}dp$. Hence, the rate of income change is, using budget exhaustion due to local nonsatiation,

$$\frac{dm}{m} = \frac{D^{\mathrm{T}}}{px}dp \qquad (7.2)$$

The right-hand side of equation (7.2) matches the Divisia index (7.1). This completes the proof that the Divisia index measures the rate of income change required to maintain the standard of living.

How much money does the consumer need to maintain the standard of living when the price change is discrete, from vector p to vector p'? Utility changes from u to u' and the answer is the change in expenditure to maintain utility level u, $\frac{e(p',u)-m}{m}$, which is the compensating variation as a percentage of the budget. Here, in the numerator, the compensating variation is $\int_p^{p'} \frac{\partial e(p'',u)}{\partial p''}dp'' = \int_p^{p'} D^c(p'', u)dp''$. The base situation, with price p and utility level u, is the point of reference. Had we used the current situation, with price p' and utility level u', as reference, then the role of the compensating variation would be played by the equivalent variation. Consumer's surplus is a compromise when demand is normal, as discussed in Chapter 4. Moreover, it tracks utility under conditions which will be discussed in Chapters 8 and 9. However, the simplest example is that of homothetic utility and that will be previewed now.

When utility is homothetic (which ensures local nonsatiation and, therefore, budget exhaustion), so is demand. In fact, by equation (2.3), $x = D(p, m) = D(p, 1)m$. It follows that the Divisia index (7.2) integrates to

$$\int_p^{p'} \frac{D^{\mathrm{T}}(p'', m)}{m}dp'' = \int_p^{p'} D^{\mathrm{T}}(p, 1)dp'' \qquad (7.3)$$

This is consumer's surplus normalized by income. Because of the homotheticity and the consequent independence, the line integral of the Divisia index is path independent, see Proposition 4.1.

We will now discuss the relationship between price indices and the expenditure function. As a preliminary, recall equation (2.5): $e(p, u) = e(p, 1)u$. This equation shows expenditure as being proportional to the standard of living, and that the proportionality coefficient is a function of price. We may say that $e(p, 1)$ is a price level index. The Divisia index, however, measures the growth rate, i.e. the derivative of $\ln e(p, 1)$. Here, the change of the cost-of-living index is independent of u, by the presumed linear homogeneity of utility. More formally, the relationship is as follows.

The point of departure is that ordinary demand, which depends on the budget m, and compensated demand, which depends on the utility level u, have the same value if the budget equals the expenditure required to attain the utility level, in other words if $m = e(p, u)$. Thus, $D(p, e(p, u)) = D^c(p, u)$. Under linear homogeneity, this equality becomes $e(p, u)D(p, 1) = uD^c(p, 1)$ and, further, $ue(p, 1)D(p, 1) = uD^c(p, 1)$. u cancels out and we obtain $e(p, 1)D(p, 1) = D^c(p, 1)$. In other words, ordinary demand and compensated demand are collinear, and the proportionality coefficient is the cost of one util, $e(p, 1)$. Divisia index (7.3) can now be written $\int_p^{p'} \frac{D^{cT}(p,1)}{e(p,1)} dp''$. The primitive function of the integrand is $\ln e(p, 1)$, using the chain rule and Shephard's lemma (Chapter 2). This proves that the Divisia index, (7.2), is the derivative of $\ln e(p, 1)$, and that the integrated Divisia index, (7.3), equals

$$\ln e(p', 1) - \ln e(p, 1) \tag{7.4}$$

Summarizing, we have three ways to measure inflation. First, there is the local Divisia measure, (7.1) or the right-hand side of (7.2). Second, there is consumer's surplus normalized by income, (7.3). Third, there is the constant-utility expenditure growth rate, (7.4) or the left-hand side of (7.2). The formulas are equivalent if utility is homothetic. This assumption will be relaxed in Chapters 8 and 9. The Divisia index is an exact measure of a local change, dp. It has the beauty that only price changes and expenditure shares are needed. However, it should be acknowledged that this appealing feature does not hold when discrete changes are measured, say over a year. Then global properties are relevant, such as the functional form and the parameters of the expenditure function, or, at a more fundamental and econometrically difficult level, of the utility function.

A good example is the price index analysis based on the CES function, which was introduced and analyzed in Chapter 5. From equation (5.7), we have the CES price level index, namely $I(p) = e(p,1) = (\sum_{i=1}^{n} \alpha_i^\sigma p_i^{1-\sigma})^{1/(1-\sigma)}$. This index requires knowledge of the elasticity of substitution, σ, unlike the Divisia index and the two main discrete time indices, the Laspeyres and the Paasche indices, which will be defined in the following equation (7.5). Such differences between cost-of-living indices play a role in wage negotiations and, therefore, are worth exploring.

Here we go. The price vector changes from base p to current p' and the idea of a price index is to track the value change of a commodity bundle. The Divisia index analyzes the infinitesimal change from p to $p + dp$ and the relevant commodity bundle is the instantaneous quantity vector x. In discrete time, however, we must deal with two commodity bundles, namely x and x'. Choice of the first commodity bundle, x, defines the Laspeyres index, denoted L, and choice of the second bundle, x', defines the Paasche index, denoted P. Formally,

$$L = p'x/px, P = p'x'/px' \qquad (7.5)$$

To compare the Laspeyres and Paasche indices, consider the CES demand function. Then, by equation (5.11), $x_i = \frac{(\alpha_i/p_i)^\sigma m}{\alpha_1^\sigma p_1^{1-\sigma}+\cdots+\alpha_i^\sigma p_i^{1-\sigma}+\cdots+\alpha_n^\sigma p_n^{1-\sigma}}$, and likewise for current demand, i.e. with x and p primed. The denominator is the same for all i and may be ignored when substituting in equation (7.5) (where x is present in the numerator and in the denominator). Thus, equation (7.5) becomes

$$L = \frac{\sum_{i=1}^{n} p_i'(\alpha_i/p_i)^\sigma}{\sum_{i=1}^{n} p_i(\alpha_i/p_i)^\sigma}, \quad P = \frac{\sum_{i=1}^{n} p_i'(\alpha_i/p_i')^\sigma}{\sum_{i=1}^{n} p_i(\alpha_i/p_i')^\sigma} \qquad (7.6)$$

The Laspeyres and Paasche indices measure the current price level (p') relative to the base price level (p) and, therefore, must

be contrasted with the ratio of the current to the base CES price
level indices (5.7), as follows:

$$\frac{I(p')}{I(p)} = \left(\frac{\sum_{i=1}^{n} p'_i (\alpha_i/p'_i)^\sigma}{\sum_{i=1}^{n} p_i (\alpha_i/p_i)^\sigma}\right)^{1/(1-\sigma)} \tag{7.7}$$

It is illuminating to consider a special case of the CES func-
tion, namely the Cobb–Douglas function, $U(x) = x_1^{\alpha_1} \dots x_n^{\alpha_n}$,
with $\alpha_1 + \cdots + \alpha_n = 1$. Then the elasticity of substitution is
$\sigma = 1$ according to Table 5.1, and, by equation (5.11) (where
the denominator is 1), the quantities demanded are

$$x_i = \alpha_i m/p_i \tag{7.8}$$

Hence, utility is

$$u = (\alpha_1 m/p_1)^{\alpha_1} \cdots (\alpha_n m/p_n)^{\alpha_n} = (\alpha_1/p_1)^{\alpha_1} \cdots (\alpha_n/p_n)^{\alpha_n} m \tag{7.9}$$

and, for future reference, the logarithm of utility is

$$v = \ln m + \alpha_1 \ln(\alpha_1/p_1) - \cdots - \alpha_n \ln(\alpha_n/p_n) \tag{7.10}$$

Solving equation (7.9) for m, $I(p) = e(p,1) = (p_1/\alpha_1)^{\alpha_1} \cdots (p_n/\alpha_n)^{\alpha_n}$. Consequently, the Cobb–Douglas variant of price index (7.7) is

$$\frac{I(p')}{I(p)} = \left(\frac{p'_1}{p_1}\right)^{\alpha_1} \cdots \left(\frac{p'_n}{p_n}\right)^{\alpha_n} \tag{7.11}$$

The Laspeyres and Paasche indices (7.6) are proxies for
the exact indices (7.7) or (7.11). Not surprisingly, if all prices
increase at the same rate, all these indices are equal to this rate,
as can be easily verified. However, if the price development is
unequal, the indices deviate. The Laspeyres index sticks to the
base period quantities and does not consider that consumers
substitute out commodities that become more expensive. For
this reason, the Laspeyres index overstates the exact index.

By the same reasoning, the Paasche index understates the exact index.

I illustrate this for the unequal price development from $p_1 = p_2 = 1$ to $p_1' = 1$ and $p_2 = p$, and parameters $\alpha = \beta = \sigma = 1/2$. Equations (7.6) and (7.7) reduce to $L = 1/2(1 + p)$, $P = (1 + p/\sqrt{p})/(1 + 1/\sqrt{p})$, $I(p')/I(p) = [1/2(1 + \sqrt{p})]2$. The gap between the Laspeyres and the exact indices is $L - I(p')/I(p) = 1/2(1 + p) - [1/2(1 + \sqrt{p})]2 = 1/2 + 1/2p - 1/4 - 1/2\sqrt{p} - 1/4p = 1/4(1 + 2\sqrt{p} + p) = 1/4(1 + \sqrt{p})^2 \geq 0$, confirming that the Laspeyres index overstates. The ratio of the exact to the Paasche indices is $1/4(1 + \sqrt{p})2/[(1 + \sqrt{p})/(1 + 1/\sqrt{p})] = 1/4(1 + \sqrt{p})(1 + 1/\sqrt{p}) = 1/4(2 + \sqrt{p} + 1/\sqrt{p})$. This ratio exceeds 1 if and only if $\sqrt{p} + 1/\sqrt{p} \geq 2$ or $p + 1 - 2\sqrt{p} \geq 0$, which is always true because the left-hand side equals a square, namely $(\sqrt{p} - 1)^2$. This confirms that the Paasche index understates.

A reasonable empirical value for the elasticity of substitution is $\sigma = 0.7$. See Shapiro and Wilcox (1996). They estimate that the consumer price index, which is Laspeyres-based, overstates the true cost-of-living inflation by 1.0 percentage point per year. This result is significant for wage, social security, and pension indexing.

Since the Laspeyres index overestimates and the Paasche index underestimates the true price index, a pragmatic alternative is the geometric mean of the two. The *Fisher index* is defined by $P_F = \sqrt{(P_L P_P)}$. The Fisher index has some nice properties. The most important one is that *the price change looking back from the current period to the base period is the reciprocal*. When the price index climbs 25% between periods b and c from 1.00 to 1.25, it better reduces by 20% from 1.25 to 1.00 or from 1.00 to 0.80 when looking back. The Laspeyres and the Paasche indices fail this test, but the Fischer index passes it.

The Fisher index is a pragmatic measure, but it is not grounded in consumer's well-being theory. The Divisia index also looks mechanical, but we have seen it is tightly connected to the concept of consumer's surplus, remember equation (7.3), and as announced, it holds the promise of being modifiable in ways that makes it utility tracking in different situations, not just the simple one where utility functions are homothetic, meaning that income effects are absent and Engel curves are straight lines radiating from the origin. In the next chapter, Chapter 8, we modify the concept of consumer's surplus slightly, defining the consumer's index, of which several variants will be presented and analyzed so as to accommodate income effects and even nonlinear Engel curves. We will return to various demand systems known from the literature in Chapter 9.

Chapter 8

The Consumer's Index: Theory

Consumer's surplus has a bad reputation as a measure of consumer's well-being. It is considered an approximation of other measures, namely of the equivalent variation and of the compensating variation. The latter two measures are called exact in the literature; see the review in Chapter 1. The terminology of 'exact' and 'approximation' is suggestive, favoring the variations and casting a shadow of doubt over the concept of consumer's surplus. The aim of this book is to shake up this perception. Yes, I find it is the opposite. In my view, consumer's surplus is the superior concept. Okay, consumer's surplus has a defect — it does not track utility when income varies — but the defect can be fixed by minor modifications, which make consumer's surplus dimensionless and utility tracking. This revision of consumer's surplus defines the so-called consumer's index (ten Raa, 2020) and is the subject of this chapter. The known result that the consumer's index tracks utility for homothetic utility functions will be explained. Moreover, this chapter will demonstrate that the consumer's index tracks utility even for some nonhomothetic utility functions, a feature that potentially opens new applications, which will be discussed in Chapter 9.

But first let us review the concept of homotheticity. In Chapter 2, a (utility) function U was defined *homothetic* if it is a monotonic transformation of a homogeneous function. Formally,

$U(x) = f(h(x))$, where x is an n-dimensional (commodity) vector, h is a homogeneous function of degree $d > 0$, and f is an increasing function. Homogeneity of degree d is defined by the condition that function h fulfills $h(sx) = s^d h(x)$ for any positive scalar s. Without loss of generality, we may assume that the homogeneity is of degree $d = 1$, which is also called linear homogeneity. The proof of this statement is as follows.

Let function U be homothetic, then there is a $d > 0$ such that $U(x) = f(h(x))$ with $h(sx) = s^d h(x)$. Define function $\hat{U}$ by $\hat{U}(x) = h(x)^{1/d}$. Then $U(x) = f(h(x)) = f(\hat{U}(x)^d) = f(g(\hat{U}(x)))$, where function g is defined by $g(y) = y^d$ for scalars y. U is a transformation of $\hat{U}$ by means of the composition of g and f. This transformation is increasing because g and f are increasing (and the composition of increasing functions is increasing). Function $\hat{U}$ fulfills $\hat{U}(sx) = h(sx)^{1/d} = [s^d h(x)]^{1/d} = sh(x)^{1/d} = s\hat{U}(x)$, hence is linearly homogeneous. This completes the proof that we may assume linear homogeneity.

A second assumption we may make, also without loss of generality, is that for a homothetic utility function the monotonic transformation is the natural logarithm. The proof of this statement is as follows.

Let utility function U be homothetic, then, as we have just seen $U(x) = f(\hat{U}(x))$ with $\hat{U}(sx) = s\hat{U}(x)$ and f an increasing function. Since U is a utility function, we may take an increasing transformation of U. For the transformation, take the composition of f^{-1} and $\ln$, which is increasing indeed. Then U is transformed to $\ln \hat{U}$, where $\hat{U}$ is linearly homogeneous. This completes the proof that we may assume the monotonic transformation is the natural logarithm.

Summarizing, a homothetic utility function can be written as

$$\ln U(x) : U(sx) = sU(x)(s > 0) \tag{8.1}$$

Utility homotheticity (8.1) has three consequences.

The first consequence is that *expenditure is linearly homogeneous in utility*. Here is the proof. By definition (2.2), expenditure $e(p, s)$ minimizes $px : U(x) \geq s$ or, by the equality in (8.1), $U(x/s) \geq 1$. The solution is x/s with $px/s = e(p, 1)$ or $e(p, s) = px = se(p, 1)$.

The second consequence of utility homotheticity is that *demand is proportional to the budget*. Here is the proof. By Shephard's lemma (Chapter 2) and the first consequence (the linear homogeneity of expenditure in utility), we have $x = D(p, m) = D^c(p, U(x)) = \frac{\partial e}{\partial p}(p, U(x)) = \frac{\partial e}{\partial p}(p, mU(x/m)) = m\frac{\partial e}{\partial p}(p, U(x/m)) = mD^c(p, U(x/m)) = mD(p, px/m) = mD(p, 1)$. In other words, demand is multiplicatively separable in price and income.

The third consequence of homotheticity is that *logarithmic indirect utility*,

$$v(p, m) = \ln V(p, m) = \ln U(D(p, m)) \tag{8.2}$$

is *additively separable*:

$$v(p, m) = v(p, 1) + \ln m \tag{8.3}$$

The proof of equation (8.3) is straightforward. By the proportionality of (homothetic utility driven) demand, (8.2) becomes $v(p, m) = \ln U(D(p, m)) = \ln U(mD(p, 1)) = \ln U(D(p, 1)) + \ln m = v(p, 1) + \ln m$.

We have laid the groundwork of homothetic utility functions and will now pursue the analysis of consumer's well-being. The analysis begins with an application of Roy's lemma (Chapter 2): $D(p, m) = -\frac{\partial v}{\partial p} / \frac{\partial v}{\partial m}$. Multiplying through by the marginal utility of money, $\frac{\partial v}{\partial m} = 1/m$ according to equation (8.3), the price effect on indirect homothetic utility is seen to be

$$\frac{\partial v(p, m)}{\partial p} = -\frac{D(p, m)}{m}, \quad \frac{\partial v(p, m)}{\partial m} = \frac{1}{m} \tag{8.4}$$

The first term in equation (8.4) is the vector of partial derivatives of indirect utility with respect to the commodity price components.

Let us first analyze the pure price effect on the consumer, that is keeping the budget fixed. According to equation (8.4), the effect of a price change from p to p' is

$$v(p', m) - v(p, m) = \int_p^{p'} \frac{\partial v(p'', m)}{\partial p''} dp'' = -\int_p^{p'} \frac{D(p'', m)}{m} dp''$$

$$(8.5)$$

Equation (8.4) tells that the change in homothetic utility due to a price change equals the integral of demand, i.e. the variation of consumer's surplus (4.2), normalized by income m. The result generalizes equation (6.3) obtained for CES functions. The normalized consumer's surplus is an exact measure, not the Hicksian measures of equivalent variation and compensating variation. Strictly speaking this conclusion has been derived for homothetic utility functions and constant income, but the analysis goes further. First, we consider simultaneous price and income changes and then we consider nonhomothetic utility functions.

Let the price–budget combination change from (p, m) to (p', m'). The additive separability of the price and income effects (8.3) is powerful: The price effect on utility is $v(p', 1) - v(p, 1)$. By the same equation (8.3), this price effect equals $v(p', m) - v(p, m)$, i.e. (8.5). Indeed, by the multiplicative separability of demand, $D(p'', m)/m$ on the right side of (8.5) is independent of m. Hence the price effect of the change from (p, m) to (p', m') is given by equation (8.5) where on the right side m can be replaced by any value m''. According to equation (8.3) the income effect is equal to $\ln m' - \ln m = \int_m^{m'} \frac{dm''}{m''}$. The price and income effects sum to

$$v(p', m') - v(p, m) = \int_{(p, m)}^{(p', m')} \frac{dm'' - D(p'', m'')dp''}{m''} \qquad (8.6)$$

Definition: The *consumer's index* is the change of income minus the integral of demand, normalized by income,

$$CI = \int_{(p,m)}^{(p',m')} \frac{dm'' - D(p'',m'')dp''}{m''}.$$

The consumer's index (ten Raa, 2020) is the difference between the logarithmic growth factor of income — $\ln(m'/m)$ — and the income normalized variation of consumer's surplus (4.2). Since the variation of consumer's surplus measures the reduction of consumer's well-being, the inclusion of the minus sign involved with the taking of the difference in the definition of the consumer's index makes this measure of well-being decrease when a price goes up, as should be. In addition, the consumer's index incorporates the income rise, but in logarithmic fashion.

For homothetic utility functions, the second term in equation (8.6), the price integral, is independent of m'', and, therefore, the consumer's index reduces to

$$CI = v(p',m') - v(p,m) = \ln(m'/m) - \int_p^{p'} D(p'',1)dp'' \quad (8.7)$$

Equations (8.6) and (8.7) show that the consumer's index not only tracks utility, but in fact equals the variation of utility. The derivation of equation (8.6) used equation (8.5) for the price effect on utility. In turn, equation (8.5) used equation (8.4), Roy's lemma, for a homothetic utility function, with marginal utility of money $1/m$. Hence, the conclusion that equation (8.6) shows that the consumer's index measures the variation of utility is warranted for homothetic utility functions.

As a prime example, and for future use, let us evaluate the consumer's index for Cobb–Douglas demands, $x_i = \alpha_i m/p_i$ (7.8) (where the coefficients are clearly the budget shares), with logarithmic utility $v = \ln m + \alpha_1 \ln(\alpha_1/p_1) - \cdots - \alpha_n \ln(\alpha_n/p_n)$ (7.10). By definition and using equation (8.6), the consumer's index is

$$CI = \ln(m'/m) - \alpha_1 \ln(p_1'/p_1) - \cdots - \alpha_n \ln(p_n'/p_n) \qquad (8.8)$$

Equation (8.8) shows that for Cobb–Douglas demand the consumer's index is log linear in income and price, with weights of the latter equal to the Cobb–Douglas parameters, i.e., the budget shares.

Before we analyze nonhomothetic utility functions, let me explain that the consumer's index, though a close cousin, is a better measure than the variation of consumer's surplus, even for homothetic utility functions.

Both consumer's surplus and the consumer's index are path integrals, but in the case of consumer's surplus the integral is path dependent, even for homothetic utility functions, whereas in the case of the consumer's index the integral is not path dependent, as will be shown now. Let us consider again a consumer with a homothetic utility function facing a price–budget change from (p, m) to (p', m'). The consumer's surplus-based index of well-being is $m' - m + CS(p', m') - CS(p, m)$ (6.2). The first two terms resulted from integrating dm in utility changes equation (4.5), and the last two terms from integrating $-D(p, m)dp$, also in equation (4.5). However, in Chapter 6, the discussion of (6.2), we saw that the index depended on the path of integration from (p, m) to (p', m') and we took pains at finding the path that measures the consumer's surplus-based index correctly. The consumer's index features two revisions of consumer's surplus. First, demand is normalized by income, and second, the budget change in (8.6) is in logarithmic form. The value of the integral is path independent for homothetic utility, simply because equation (8.5) shows the value always equals $v(p, 1) - v(p', 1)$.

Indeed, we have seen in Chapter 6 that consumer's surplus does not track utility when price and income vary simultaneously. The consumer's index, however, does track utility, by equation (8.6), at least when the utility function is homothetic.

Now let us analyze the measurement of well-being for consumer's with nonhomothetic utility functions. Homotheticity can be characterized by the condition that Engel curves are linear and radiate from the origin. The effect of an income change on demand is fixed; the change of demand is in the same direction as that of demand itself. A generalization that accommodates a change of demand in any direction is that of quasi-homotheticity. This property is characterized by the condition that Engel curves are linear but not necessarily going through the origin. From a local (i.e. first-order) perspective, this is a full generalization. Yet, we will derive the important result that the consumer's index continues to track utility.

Engel curves plot the demand points for varying levels of income m but fixed price vectors p. Quasi-homotheticity is characterized by the condition that Engel curves are linear, but going through an arbitrary commodity bundle, not necessarily the origin. The term quasi-homotheticity is relatively recent, but the idea goes back to Gorman (1953, 1961). The commodity bundle that the Engel curve intersects may depend on the price vector p, since that is fixed for each Engel curve, and is denoted $f(p)$, following Gorman (1961). Due to this price dependence, the Engel curves need not intersect a common commodity bundle. The direction in which demand changes as m increases is denoted $g(p)$. Demand is $f(p)$ plus a multiple of $g(p)$. Clearly, the greater the multiple, the more the utility. In fact, for the coefficient of $g(p)$ one can take the utility level, provided that the $f(p)$s are selected on the Engel curves such that they carry a common base level of utility, i.e. the $f(p)$s form an indifference surface, typically (but not necessarily) the lowest or *base* one, also called the *subsistence utility*, which can and will be normalized at 0, and provided that the magnitude of each $g(p)$ is selected such that the additional utilities they carry also have a common value, which will be normalized at 1. In short, *quasi-homotheticity* is defined by the condition that compensated demand is of the form

$$D^c(p, u) = f(p) + ug(p), U(f(p)) = 0 \qquad (8.9)$$

For each price p, there is a linear relationship between income and utility. The essence of quasi-homotheticity is that compensated demand is linear in utility, hence demand is linear in income. Here, linearity is to be understood in the sense that the graph is straight but does not necessarily go through the origin of the commodity space. In fact, the graph intersects $f(p)$ and, as said, this commodity bundle need not be fixed.

Let us derive the demand function associated with quasi-homotheticity. The trick is to first derive the expenditure function. Now premultiplying quasi-homotheticity condition (8.9) by p, introducing Stahl's (1983) shorthands for incremental expenditures, $A(p) = pg(p)$, and for base expenditures $B(p) = pf(p)$ (needed to support the subsistence utility), we obtain the expenditure function,

$$m = e(p, u) = B(p) + uA(p) \qquad (8.10)$$

Inversion of equation (8.10) yields indirect utility

$$V(p, m) = \frac{m - B(p)}{A(p)} \qquad (8.11)$$

Differentiating the expenditure function of equation (8.10), Shephard's lemma (Chapter 2), yields $D^c(p, u) = \frac{\partial e}{\partial p}(p, u) = \frac{\partial B}{\partial p} + u\frac{\partial A}{\partial p}$. Substituting equation (8.11) for utility, we find that *quasi-homotheticity* yields the following demand function:

$$D(p, m) = \frac{\partial B}{\partial p} + \frac{m - B(p)}{A(p)} \frac{\partial A}{\partial p} \qquad (8.12)$$

Equation (8.12) can be found in Stahl (1983), albeit without the derivation. Demand (8.12) is called PIGL demand, a term coined by Muellbauer (1975, 1976). PIGL stands for 'price independent generalized linearity.' Whatever the price, demand is linear in the budget. The essence of PIGL demand is linearity in m with the coefficient and the constant term being functions of p. The coefficient of m, $\frac{1}{A(p)}\frac{\partial A}{\partial p} = \frac{\partial \ln A}{\partial p}$, determines A, by integration of the coefficient and plugging the consequent $\ln A$ in the exponential function. Subsequently, the constant term, $\frac{\partial B}{\partial p} - \frac{B(p)}{A(p)}\frac{\partial A}{\partial p}$, determines B, by solving the differential equation.

For homothetic utility, Roy's lemma (Chapter 2) implied that the variation of income normalized consumer's surplus tracks utility, see equation (8.5). That analysis is now extended to the case of quasi-homotheticity. By Roy's lemma and equation (8.11), respectively: $\frac{\partial V}{\partial p} = -D(p,m)\frac{\partial V}{\partial m}$ and $\frac{\partial V}{\partial m} = 1/A(p) = \frac{V(p,m)}{m-B(p)}$. Combining and substituting equations (8.2) and (8.12), we obtain

$$\frac{\partial v}{\partial p} = \frac{-D(p,m)}{m-B(p)}, \quad \frac{\partial v}{\partial m} = \frac{1}{m-B(p)} \qquad (8.13)$$

Equation (8.13) displays the price and income effects on indirect quasi-homothetic utility and generalizes equation (8.4) for homothetic utility. Indeed, when utility is homothetic, the commodity bundle that the Engel curve intersects is the origin, $f(p) = 0$, so that $B(p) = pf(p) = 0$ and, therefore, $\frac{\partial v}{\partial p} = \frac{-D(p,m)}{m}$, $\frac{\partial v}{\partial m} = \frac{1}{m}$. Integrating, we obtained the consumer's index, see equation (8.6) and the definition there. Equation (8.13) suggests the following generalization of the consumer's index.

Definition: The *generalized consumer's index* is the change of income minus the integral of demand, normalized by excess income,

$$CI = \int_{(p,m)}^{(p',m')} \frac{dm'' - D(p'',m'')dp''}{m'' - B(p'')}.$$

The generalized consumer's index generalizes the consumer's index, because homotheticity is the case where $B(p) = 0$. This further generalization of consumer's surplus preserves the tracking of quasi-homothetic utility (now by CI), as will be demonstrated in what follows.

The path independence of generalized consumer's index for quasi-homothetic utility can be demonstrated by explicit evaluation of the integral. Substituting equation (8.12), the generalized consumer's index becomes

$$
\begin{aligned}
CI &= \int_{(p,m)}^{(p',m')} \left[\frac{dm''}{m'' - B(p'')} - \frac{\frac{\partial B}{\partial p} + \frac{m'' - B(p'')}{A(p'')} \frac{\partial A}{\partial p}}{m'' - B(p'')} dp'' \right] \\
&= \int_{(p,m)}^{(p',m')} \left[\frac{dm'' - \frac{\partial B}{\partial p} dp''}{m'' - B(p'')} - \frac{\frac{\partial A}{\partial p} dp''}{A(p'')} \right] \\
&= \int_{(p,m)}^{(p',m')} d\ln \frac{m'' - B(p'')}{A(p'')} = \int_{(p,m)}^{(p',m')} d\ln V(p'', m'') \\
&= \int_{(p,m)}^{(p',m')} dv(p'', m''),
\end{aligned}
$$

by equations (8.11) and change of utility variable (8.2). In short,

$$
CI = v(p', m') - v(p, m) \tag{8.14}
$$

Equation (8.14) shows that the natural logarithm of indirect utility, v, is a potential function of the integrand of the generalized consumer's index. The generalized consumer's index tracks quasi-homothetic utility, in fact the generalized consumer's index equals the variation of logarithmic utility.

The *generalized consumer's index* was called the generalized Divisia quantity index by Stahl (1983) and claimed to be *path independent if and only if preferences are quasi-homothetic.* The if part (the sufficiency of quasi-homotheticity) is valid, as we have just seen by explicit evaluation of the integral. The only if part (the necessity of quasi-homotheticity) is established now. The generalized consumer's index is defined by demand D and base expenditure B. Quasi-homotheticity is defined by compensated demand (8.8) or, equivalently, ordinary (8.12).

So, we must show that path independence in the generalized consumer's index implies (8.12).

A line integral of the form $\int_x^{x'} h(x'')dx''$ is path independent (if and) only if the matrix of partial derivatives of h is symmetric. In the generalized consumer's index, the variable is $x = (p, m)$ and the function is $h(p, m) = \left(\frac{-D}{m-B(p)} \quad \frac{1}{m-B(p)}\right)$. Symmetry of the matrix of partial derivatives means $\frac{\partial}{\partial p}\frac{1}{m-B(p)} = \frac{\partial}{\partial m}\frac{-D(p,m)}{m-B(p)}$. (For the same reason, $\frac{\partial}{\partial p}\frac{D(p,m)}{m-B(p)}$ is also symmetric, but that will not be needed in the derivation of homotheticity.) Carrying out the two differentiations (with respect to p on the left-hand side and with respect to m on the right-hand side) and then multiplying through by $[m - B(p)]^2$, $\frac{\partial B(p)}{\partial p} = -[m - B(p)]\frac{\partial D(p,m)}{\partial m} + D(p, m)$. For each p, this is an ordinary differential equation for $D(p, m)$ with respect to m. The solution is linear in m, namely $D(p, m) = \frac{\partial B(p)}{\partial p} + [m - B(p)]\frac{\partial D[p,B(p)]}{\partial m}$. To conclude that demand is quasi-homothetic, i.e. (8.10), it remains to show that $\frac{\partial D(p,B(p))}{\partial m} = \frac{\partial \ln A(p)}{\partial p}$ for some function A, i.e. that there exists a potential function for the demand income effect of the form $\ln A$. We use the fact that D is a demand function. It generates an expenditure function e, see Chapter 2. Shephard's lemma, differentiated with respect to u in $u = 0$, see (8.7), yields $\frac{\partial^2 e(p,0)}{\partial p\partial u} = \frac{\partial D^c(p,0)}{\partial u} = \frac{\partial D(p,B(p))}{\partial m}\frac{\partial e(p,0)}{\partial u}$, or defining $A(p) = \frac{\partial e(p,0)}{\partial u}$, $\frac{\partial A(p)}{\partial p} = \frac{\partial D(p,B(p))}{\partial m}A(p)$. This completes the proof that quasi-homotheticity is necessary for path independence of line integral *CI*.

The path independence of the generalized consumer's index makes it a well-defined measure. Moreover, it tracks utility. These findings hold for quasi-homothetic demands, but, as Gorman (1976, p. 232) writes, quasi-homotheticity 'is important because sufficiently smooth preferences can always be approximated quasi-homothetically in a given neighborhood, just as their Engel curves can be by straight lines.' Hence, the results are useful, and I will discuss various specifications in Chapter 9.

The local approximation of smooth preferences by quasi-homothetic preferences can be repeated in a next neighborhood. This is best explained at the level of compensated demand functions, $D^c(p, u) = f(p) + ug(p), U(f(p)) = 0$ (8.9). Let this hold for the neighborhood $0 \leq u \leq u'$. For $u \geq u'$, let $D^c(p, u) = f(p) + u'g(p) + (u - u')h(p)$. Premultiplication by p yields the expenditure function, and Shephard's lemma (Chapter 2) yields demand. In the region $0 \leq u \leq u'$, we have quasi-homotheticity with base utility indifference surface formed by the $f(p)$'s and linear Engel curves in the directions $g(p)$. In the region $u \geq u'$, we have quasi-homotheticity with base utility indifference surface formed by the $f(p) + u'g(p)$s and linear Engel curves in the directions $h(p)$. In each region, generalized consumer's index CI can be used to measure consumer's well-being. And the changes with a path crossing both regions can be added. This technique can be extended to a piecemeal quasi-linear demand function, with more than two pieces.

Another interesting extension of the analysis is from individual consumers to market demand. Consider two consumers, a and b, with quasi-homothetic utility functions. Then, by equation (8.9),

$$D_a^c(p, u_a) = f_a(p) + u_a g_a(p), \quad U_a(f_a(p)) = 0,$$
$$D_b^c(p, u_b) = f_b(p) + u_b g_b(p), \quad U_b(f_b(p)) = 0 \qquad (8.15)$$

Gorman (1953) assumes the Engel curves are parallel across consumers for each price p, i.e.

$$g_a = g_b = g \qquad (8.16)$$

Summation of (8.15) and substitution of (8.16) yields that aggregate compensated demand is $D^c(p, u_a, u_b) = D_a^c(p, u_a) + D_a^c(p, u_a) = f_a(p) + f_b(p) + (u_a + u_b)g(p) = f(p) + ug(p)$, where $f(p) = f_a(p) + f_b(p)$ and $u = u_a + u_b$. Hence, aggregate demand is also quasi-homothetic and can be viewed as generated by a 'representative' consumer with base indifference surface formed by the $f(p)$s and respective Engel curve directions $g(p)$. We see that $D^c(p, u_a, u_b)$ is a function of price p and utilitarian $u = u_a + u_b$. There is no reason to accept the utility of the representative consumer as a welfare function because it ignores distributional issues.

There is an interesting reversal of this line of thought. Suppose aggregate demand admits a generalized consumer's index that is well-defined, i.e. is path independent. Then aggregate demand must fulfill the necessary condition of path independence, i.e. quasi-homotheticity: $D^c(p, u) = f(p) + ug(p)$. Here, u is some aggregate of u_a and u_b. If $u_a = u_b = 0$, then $D^c(p, 0) = f(p) = f_a(p) + f_b(p)$. In the point $u_a = u_b = 0$, the rate of change of $D^c(p, u)$ with respect to u_a or u_b is $g(p)$, which is independent of the consumer (a or b). Hence, $D_a^c(p, u_a) = f_a(p) + u_a g(p)$ and $D_b^c(p, u_b) = f_b(p) + u_b g(p)$. Hence, both consumers must have quasi-linear demands, with the same direction of the Engel curve, $g(p)$.

Of course, there is nothing special in the assumption that the number of consumers is two. Summarizing, the generalized consumer's index is a well-defined measure of consumer's well-being if and only if consumers have quasi-homothetic demands with common directions of the Engel curves, $g(p)$. Since these directions depend on price only, not on utility or, equivalently, income, the Engel curves are linear. Since the directions are common to the consumers, the Engel curves are parallel. In short, the generalized consumer's index has a necessary and sufficient condition for being a well-defined measure of consumers' well-being, namely that *Engel curves must be linear and parallel*.

Gorman (1953, 1961) showed that the condition of parallel linear Engel curves is necessary and sufficient for aggregate demand to be generated by a representative consumer. For a nice account see Muellbauer (1976, Theorem 1). The condition is nowadays called the Gorman polar form. The crux of the

Gorman polar form is quasi-homotheticity. The Gorman polar form is the necessary and sufficient condition for both the existence of a representative consumer and the generalized consumer's index to be well defined. We may conclude that the generalized consumer's index has little applicability, but that is not so, as we will see in the next chapter. Moreover, also in Chapter 9, we will propose a variant of the generalized consumer's index that, though not generated by a representative consumer, is well defined and yet admits nonlinear Engel curves. Of course, if no representative consumer underlies a demand function, it may be ingenious that well-defined variants of consumer's surplus can still be constructed, but the question will arise if such constructs measure consumer well-being in any sense.

Chapter 9

The Consumer's Index: Applications and Extensions

We have seen in Chapter 8 that the consumer's index is well defined if and only if demand fulfills a perfect aggregation condition, namely that of quasi-homotheticity. In the present chapter, we will discuss cases and variants of quasi-homotheticity and the associated consumer's indices formulas, including even of demand functions with nonlinear Engel curves.

There are three levels of quasi-homotheticity. At the highest level, the most general case, quasi-homotheticity is of the form (8.9), where the $f(p)$'s form the indifference surface of subsistence utility. At the lowest level, the most special case, the subsistence surface of quasi-homotheticity collapses into the origin, and quasi-homotheticity reduces to homotheticity. At an intermediate level, the popular case in applied work, the subsistence surface collapses into some other point, subsistence bundle γ. In this case, the utility function is of the form $U(x) = \Psi(x - \gamma)$ with Ψ homothetic. Such a utility function U is a translated homothetic utility function and has two names. It is called *affinely homothetic* by Blackorby *et al.* (1978) and *trans-homothetic* by Stahl (1983).

The simplest case of an affinely homothetic utility function is a translation of the Cobb–Douglas function. Klein and Rubin (1947) introduced the associated demand functions,

$x_i = \sum_j \alpha_{ij} \frac{p_j}{p_i} + \beta_i \frac{m}{p_i}$, $i = 1, \ldots, n$. Multiplying by p_i and summing must yield m. This implies the restrictions $\sum_{i,j} \alpha_{ij} p_j = 0$ and $\sum_i \beta_i = 1$. Moreover, Slutsky symmetry (see Chapter 2) implies the restriction $\alpha_{ij} = -\beta_i \gamma_j - \delta_{ij} \gamma_i$, where the so-called Kronecker symbol $\delta_{ij} = 0$ if $i \neq j$ and $\delta_{ii} = 0$, and where I premultiplied Klein and Rubin's (1947) γ_i's by -1 for consistency with Blackorby *et al.* (1978) notation for the subsistence bundle, γ. Under these restrictions Samuelson (1947a) recovered the underlying utility function, namely $U(x) = \prod_i (x_i - \gamma_i)^{\beta_i}$, a translated Cobb–Douglas function, with subsistence bundle γ. Base expenditures $B(p)$ are simply $p\gamma$. By the well-known first-order condition of Cobb–Douglas utility maximization (and the translation change of variables), $p_i(x_i - \gamma_i) = \beta_i(m - p\gamma)$ or, solving and using obvious matrix notation, denoting the diagonal matrix obtained by placement of vector p by $\hat{p}$, $x = \hat{p}^{-1}\beta(m - p\gamma) + \gamma$. In other words, the excess expenditures, over and above the subsistence costs, are fixed shares of the budget net of the subsistence costs. Translated Cobb–Douglas demand is a form of quasi-homothetic demand (8.10), namely with coefficient $\frac{\partial A}{A(p)\partial p} = \hat{p}^{-1}\beta$ and constant term $\frac{\partial B}{\partial p} - \frac{B(p)}{A(p)}\frac{\partial A}{\partial p} = \hat{p}^{-1}\beta p\gamma + \gamma$. The coefficient determines A (by integration). The generalized consumer's index is $CI = \int_{(p,m)}^{(p',m')} \frac{dm'' - D(p'',m'')dp''}{m'' - B(p'')} = \int_{(p,m)}^{(p',m')} \frac{dm'' - [\widehat{p''}^{-1}\beta(m - p\gamma) + \gamma]dp''}{m'' - p''\gamma}$. Now recall equation (8.8): without the translation, in other words when $\gamma = 0$, the consumer's index is $\ln(m'/m) - \alpha_1 \ln(p_1'/p_1) - \cdots - \alpha_n \ln(p_n'/p_n)$. With the translation, we have a change of variable where the income variable runs from the initial excess budget to the end excess budget. Hence, the consumer's index of the translated Cobb–Douglas demand is $\ln \frac{m' - p'\gamma}{m - p\gamma} - \sum_{i=1}^n \alpha_i \ln \frac{p_i'}{p_i}$.

Stone (1954) estimated the Klein–Rubin demand functions and ever since we speak of the *Stone–Geary utility function* and the consequent *linear expenditure system*. The naming of Stone–Geary is a historical accident. Deaton (2016) notes that Stone seemed to be unaware of the utility function and Geary (1950) merely rediscovered the utility function, well after Samuelson (1947a). Deaton (2016) also notes that according to Cambridge legend, Prais and Houthakker's (1956) was the first study in economics to use an electronic computer. However, Leontief (1951) used the electronic computer successfully in 1948, see Meade (2017) and Halsmayer (2019) for interesting histories. Let me conjure that Deaton's claim is yet another instance of Cambridge legend.

Since the Cobb–Douglas function is a member of the family of CES functions (see Table 5.1), a more general affinely homothetic function is a translation of the CES function. Liao and Wang (2018) consider the consumption of the agricultural good c_a and of the non-agricultural good c_n and the utility function $\left[\omega_a(c_a - \overline{a})^{\frac{\varepsilon-1}{\varepsilon}} + \omega_n c_n^{\frac{\varepsilon-1}{\varepsilon}}\right]^{\frac{\varepsilon}{\varepsilon-1}}$, where $\varepsilon > 0$ and $\varepsilon \neq 1$. $\overline{a}$ is the subsistence parameter and ω_a and ω_n are weights. They call the function a Stone–Geary CES function (Liao and Wang, 2018). Thus, the prefix Stone–Geary stands for affine homotheticity, an intermediate case of quasi-homotheticity. Comparison with the CES formula (5.1) shows that $\frac{\varepsilon-1}{\varepsilon}$ plays the role of CES parameter ρ. The elasticity of substitution, (5.3), is therefore $\sigma = 1/(1 - \rho) = 1/\left(1 - \frac{\varepsilon-1}{\varepsilon}\right) = \varepsilon$.

Now let us write down the consumer's index measuring an agricultural price change. First, we review CES demand without the subsistence parameter. By Proposition 5.1, CES demand has income normalized variation of consumer's surplus $S_i/m = \frac{1}{1-\sigma} \ln\left\{1 + \left[\left(\frac{p_i'}{p_i}\right)^{1-\sigma} - 1\right]\frac{p_i x_i}{m}\right\}$. In Chapter 8, the consumer's index was defined as the difference between the change of income, $\ln(m'/m)$, and the income normalized variation of consumer's surplus. In other words, $CI_i = \ln(m'/m) - \frac{1}{1-\sigma} \ln\left\{1 + \left[\left(\frac{p_i'}{p_i}\right)^{1-\sigma} - 1\right]\frac{p_i x_i}{m}\right\}$. Applying this to the price of the agricultural good, taking into account the subsistence agricultural consumption, the translated CES consumer's index becomes $CI_a = \ln \frac{m' - p'_a \bar{a}}{m - p_a \bar{a}} - \frac{1}{1-\sigma} \ln \left\{ 1 + \left[\left(\frac{p'_a}{p_a} \right)^{1-\sigma} - 1 \right] \frac{p_a(c_a - \bar{a})}{m - p_a \bar{a}} \right\}$ for constant income m.

We have now encountered some applications of the Gorman polar form, which, however, impose some severe restrictions. This is especially true in the case of the simplest of quasi-homothetic demand functions, namely homothetic demands. In fact, a system of homothetic demands is of the Gorman polar form if and only if the individual demands are equal, assuming local nonsatiation. The proof of this statement is brief.

Consider two consumers, a and b. The Gorman polar form is given by equations (8.15) and (8.16). Homotheticity means $f_a = f_b = 0$. Summarizing, $D_a^c(p, u_a) = u_a g(p), D_b^c(p, u_b) = u_b g(p)$. Hence, the two compensated demands are equal. By demand equation (2.1), compensated demand equation (2.2), and the connecting sentence, the solution to the first equation also solves the second, assuming local nonsatiation. Then the two demands are equal.

The upshot of this result is that within the class of homothetic demands the consumer's index is a well-defined measure of well-being only if consumers have the same utility function. If consumers vary, the generalized consumer's index is a useful measure, but another stringent condition must hold: the individual Engel curves must be linear and parallel. However, there is a variant of the generalized consumer's index which facilitates certain nonlinear Engel curves. Thus, I will now introduce the logarithmic variant of the generalized consumer's index.

The essence of quasi-homotheticity is that compensated demand is linear in utility, hence demand is linear in income (not necessarily through the origin). The logarithmic variant (Lewbel, 1989) features demand that is linear in the logarithm of income. Instead of quasi-homothetic expenditure

$m = B(p) + uA(p)$ (8.10), we now have

$$\ln m = B(\ln p) + uA(\ln p) \qquad (9.1)$$

where vector $\ln p$ is defined component-wise.

By Shephard's lemma (Chapter 2),

$$\frac{\partial \ln e(p, u)}{\partial \ln p} = \frac{\hat{p}\partial e(p, u)}{m\partial p} = \frac{\hat{p}D^c(p, u)}{m} = \frac{\hat{p}D(p, m)}{m} = w(\ln p, \ln m)$$
$$(9.2)$$

In equation (9.2), w is the vector of budget shares, defined by the last equality. Analogous to the derivative of m with respect to p yielding demand, according to Shephard's lemma (9.2) (Chapter 2), the derivative of $\ln m$ with respect to $\ln p$ yields the budget shares.

In precisely the same way as quasi-homothetic expenditure (8.10) yielded demand (8.12) in Chapter 8, we now have that the logarithmic expenditure (9.1) yields budget shares

$$w = \frac{\partial B(\ln p)}{\partial \ln p} + \frac{\ln m - B}{A} \frac{\partial A(\ln p)}{\partial \ln p} \qquad (9.3)$$

Equation (9.3) is equation (2) of Lewbel (1989), with a correction (the inclusion of A in the denominator). Equation (9.3) can be traced back to Muellbauer (1976), equation (14). Muelbauer (1975, 1976) calls the demand PIGLOG. Why? Well, recall demand (8.12) was called PIGL in Chapter 8 and the OG extension creates LOG, accounting for the logarithmic variation. Anyway, the essence of PIGLOG demand is linearity in $\ln m$, with the coefficient and the constant term being functions of $\ln p$. The coefficient of $\ln m$ determines A (by integration). And once A is determined, the constant term determines B, as the solution of a differential equation.

The *logarithmic variant of the generalized consumer's index* is the change of the logarithm of income minus the integral of the budget shares, normalized by excess logarithmic income: $\tilde{CI} = \int_{(\ln p,\ln m)}^{(\ln p',\ln m')} \frac{d\ln m'' - w(\ln p'',\ln m'')d\ln p''}{\ln m'' - B(\ln p'')}$.

The logarithmic variant of the generalized consumer's index is also path independent. Lewbel (1989) argues this using Slutsky symmetry — showing it is identical when written in budget shares — but it is more illuminating to prove path independence by direct evaluation of the integral, as it yields utility tracking as a bonus. The evaluation of the integral is analogous to the one for quasi-homothetic utility, (8.14), and runs as follows.

Substituting (9.1) twice, (9.2) reads $w = \frac{\partial B}{\partial \ln p} + u\frac{\partial A}{\partial \ln p} = \frac{\partial B}{\partial \ln p} + \frac{\ln m - B(\ln p)}{A(\ln p)}\frac{\partial A}{\partial \ln p}$. Substituting this expression for w, the logarithmic variant of the generalized consumer's index becomes

$$\tilde{CI} = \int_{(\ln p,\ln m)}^{(\ln p',\ln m')} \left[\frac{d\ln m''}{\ln m'' - B(\ln p'')} \right.$$

$$\left. - \frac{\frac{\partial B}{\partial \ln p} + \frac{\ln m'' - B(\ln p'')}{A(\ln p'')}\frac{\partial A}{\partial \ln p}}{\ln m'' - B(\ln p'')}d\ln p'' \right]$$

$$= \int_{(\ln p,\ln m)}^{(\ln p',\ln m')} \left[\frac{d\ln m'' - \frac{\partial B}{\partial \ln p}d\ln p''}{\ln m'' - B(\ln p'')} - \frac{\frac{\partial A}{\partial \ln p}d\ln p''}{A(\ln p'')} \right]$$

$$= \int_{(\ln p,\ln m)}^{(\ln p',\ln m')} d\ln\left[\frac{\ln m'' - B(\ln p'')}{A(\ln p'')} \right].$$

Inverting equation (9.1), the logarithmic variant of the generalized consumer's index reduces to $\int_{(\ln p,\ln m)}^{(\ln p',\ln m')} d\ln V(\ln p'',$ $\ln m'') = \int_{(\ln p,\ln m)}^{(\ln p',\ln m')} dv(\ln p'', \ln m'')$, using change of utility variable (8.2). In short,

$$\tilde{CI} = v(\ln p', \ln m') - v(\ln p, \ln m) \tag{9.4}$$

Equation (9.4) shows that the natural logarithm of indirect utility as function of log price and log income, v, is a potential function of the integrand of the generalized consumer's index. The logarithmic variant of the generalized consumer's index tracks quasi-homothetic utility, in fact the logarithmic variant of the generalized consumer's index equals the variation of logarithmic utility.

Examples of PIGLOG demands (9.3) are Deaton and Muellbauer's (1980) Almost Ideal Demand System (AIDS) model, Jorgenson *et al.* (1980) exactly aggregable Translog model, and Lewbel's (1988) polynomial Integrable Almost Generalized Linear (IAGL) model. See Lewbel (1989a). The AIDS and the exactly aggregable Translog models are detailed next.

AIDS expenditure is $\ln m = \alpha_0 + \sum_{k,j} \gamma_{kj} \ln p_k \ln p_j + u\beta_0 \prod_k p_k^{\beta_k}$. This is indeed an example of PIGLOG expenditure $\ln m = B(\ln p) + uA(\ln p)$ (9.1), because the product term can be rewritten as $e^{\sum_k \beta_k \ln p_k}$, which is a function of $\ln p$ indeed. By Shephard's lemma (along with the assumption that consumers exhaust their budgets due to monotonicity of utility), AIDS demand is an example of PIGLOG demand. By equation (8.14), the generalized consumer's index equals the variation of logarithmic utility. It follows that we can simply solve the expenditure function for utility u, obtaining $u = \frac{\ln m - \alpha_0 - \sum_{k,j} \gamma_{kj} \ln p_k \ln p_j}{\beta_0 \prod_k p_k^{\beta_k}}$, evaluate u in the new situation (p', m') and in the base situation (p, m), take the difference of the logs, and thus obtain the generalized consumer's index, (9.4).

The Translog model is given by the indirect utility function $v = \ln V = \alpha_0 + \sum \alpha_i \ln \frac{p_i}{m} + \frac{1}{2} \sum_{i,j} \beta_{ij} \ln \frac{p_i}{m} \ln \frac{p_j}{m}$ with $\sum \alpha_i = -1$, $\beta_{ij} = \beta_{ji}$ (Christensen *et al.*, 1975) and the exact aggregation condition is $\sum_{i,j} \beta_{ij} = 0$ (Jorgenson *et al.*, 1980). Recall Shephard's lemma has the log variant (9.2). Roy's lemma was a consequence of Shephard's lemma and can also be written in log form, namely $w = -\frac{\partial \ln V / \partial \ln p}{\partial \ln V / \partial \ln m}$. Substituting the Translog, organizing the α_i's in vector α, the β_{ij}'s in matrix β, and the numbers 1 in summation vector ι, $w = \frac{\alpha + \beta \ln p - \beta \iota \ln m}{1 + \iota^T \beta \ln p - \iota^T \beta \iota \ln m} = \frac{\alpha + \beta \ln p - \beta \iota \ln m}{1 + \iota^T \beta \ln p}$, using the exact aggregation condition. This expression is linear in $\ln m$, with the coefficient and the constant term functions of $\ln p$, hence PIGLOG. The evaluation of the generalized consumer's index, (9.4), is by evaluation of indirect utility in the new situation (p', m') and in the base situation (p, m), and taking the difference of the logs.

We have seen that the concept of consumer's surplus is a superior measure of consumer well-being not only for demand with no income effects, but also for demands with straight Engel curves which do not radiate from the origin, and even for demands of which the Engel curves are not straight but linear in the logarithm of income. The buzz word is the Gorman polar form. The bulk of the literature defines the Gorman polar form as the condition of parallel linear Engel curves (Gorman, 1953). The excellent review by Honohan and Neary (2003) does so, and I stick to this convention. Lewbel (1987), however, writes that the Gorman polar form 'does not require that Engel curves themselves be linear in x [total expenditure], as is sometimes believed.' Lewbel takes his definition of the Gorman polar form from Gorman (1959), which indeed analyzes a wider class of demand functions than in Gorman (1953). This source difference explains the slight confusion. Anyway, Lewbel is right in that Gorman's demand analysis remains valid for demands with nonlinear Engel curves. The generality shows in our construction of the variant of the generalized consumer's index.

Parallel linear Engel curves are necessary and sufficient for the existence of a representative consumer. PIGLOG demands do not fulfill this condition. Yet, aggregate data fit the PIGLOG specification well. Lewbel (1991) analyzed this paradox in detail. He showed that if individual demands are PIGLOG and the income distribution is of a particular form, then aggregate demand is also a PIGLOG demand, including the parameter constraints implied by utility maximization (adding up, homogeneity, and Slutsky symmetry). The combination of this similarity condition across consumers and this income distribution property stands US and UK survey data (Lewbel, 1991). The upshot is that in practice the logarithmic variant of the generalized consumer's index (9.4) can be applied to aggregate data. However, a limitation is the same as of a utilitarian welfare function. When the index goes up, aggregate consumer's well-being increases, so some will be better off but others worse off, and one can infer little about Pareto efficiency. Yet, there are cases where statements can be made.

Debreu (1951) measured the efficiency of an economy by the coefficient of resource utilization, the percentage of the available resources required to attain the utility levels of the consumers, by requiring that allocations are in the better set (in the sense of Pareto). Now ten Raa (2008) freed the concept of micro data requirements by taking intersections of better sets across increasing utility functions. He showed that this is equivalent to imposing Leontief utility functions (different between consumers) and that the aggregate better set is also represented by a Leontief utility function. The coefficient of resource utilization is thus replaced by the Debreu–Diewert coefficient, which overestimates the Debreu coefficient of resource utilization, because it misses potential efficiency gains achievable by reallocations between consumers with different marginal rates of substitution. The Leontief function of aggregate consumption is a perfect aggregation result that, moreover, admits Pareto comparisons, because the better aggregate set equals the sum of the better individual sets (ten Raa, 2008, Lemma).

So far, the analysis, including all the cases of consumer's surplus and the variants of the consumer's index, are within the admittedly narrow neoclassical framework, where the well-being of the consumer is determined by the consumption of marketed goods. They miss the impact of quality-of-life conditions which are not priced, such as health and environmental indicators. More generally, not all goods and services, and certainly not all external effects are priced.

I will outline how the economic measures of consumer well-being can be extended as to accommodate indicators of non-marketed goods, which will be called non-economic indicators or attributes. The resulting measures are *broad measures* of consumer well-being. Examples are the Generalized Human Development Index (HDI) of Chakravarty (2003), the OECD Better Life Index, e.g. Mizobuchi (2014), and the 'Report on well-being in a broad sense in the Netherlands' of Statistics Netherlands (2020). The first one, the HDI, is well established in theory and encompasses other ones. So we will first review the index theory of Chakravarty, then introduce various broad measures, and then relate them to our framework of equivalent and compensating variations and the consumer's index.

Chakravarty (2003) assumes that there are k attributes of well-being. These attributes may be life expectancy at birth, real GDP per capita, educational attainment, housing, provision of public goods, and so on. Let x_i stand for the attainment level or the value of attribute i for the country under consideration, where $i = 1, 2, \ldots, k$. Denote the lower and upper bounds of x_i by m_i and M_i, respectively. An indicator for i is a real-valued function A that associates a value $A(x_i, m_i, M_i)$. Theorem 1 of Chakravarty (2003) shows that a set of five index axioms implies that the indicators are

$$A(x_i, m_i, M_i) = f((x_i - m_i)/(M_i - m_i)) \qquad (9.5)$$

where f is an increasing, strictly concave function on the unit interval with $f(0) = 0$ and $f(1) = 1$. The five index axioms under which (9.5) follows are *normalization*: $A(x_i, m_i, M_i) = 0$ if $x_i = m_i$ and $= 1$ if $x_i = M_i$; *monotonicity*: A is increasing in

x_i; *translation invariance*: $A(x_i, m_i, M_i) = A(x_i + c, m_i + c, M_i + c)$, where c is any scalar such that $m_i + c \geq 0$; *homogeneity*: $A(x_i, m_i, M_i) = A(cx_i, cm_i, cM_i)$ for any $c > 0$; and *lower gain in indicator at higher levels of attainment difference*: indicator gain $A(x_i + \delta, m_i, M_i) - A(x_i, m_i, M_i)$ is decreasing in δ. The lower gain axiom drives the strict concavity of the indicator and is often relaxed to a non-higher gain axiom. Then the indicator is just concave, not necessarily strictly.

The indicator values of (9.5), call them a_i — residing between 0 and 1 by (9.5) — are aggregated by indicator function I with values $I(a_1, \ldots, a_k)$ — also to reside between 0 and 1. Theorem 3 of Chakravarty (2003) shows that a set of three axioms implies that the aggregate indicator is

$$I(a_1, \ldots, a_k) = \sum_{i=1}^{k} a_i/k \qquad (9.6)$$

The three aggregation axioms under which (9.6) follows are *normalization*: $I(z, \ldots, z) = z$; *consistency in aggregation*: $I(a_1 + b_1, \ldots, a_k + b_k) = I(a_1, \ldots, a_k) + I(b_1, \ldots, b_k)$; and *symmetry* (SYM): insensitivity of I to permutation of its arguments. If all five plus three axioms are accepted, (9.5) can be substituted in a_i of (9.6).

The Human Development Index (HDI) is described in and discussed by Klugman *et al.* (2011). The attributes are living standard, health, and education. Living standard is measured by gross domestic product per capita, health is measured by life expectancy, and education by literacy and gross enrollment ratio. The two dimensions of education make the number of attributes $k = 4$. The lower and upper bounds (m_i, M_i) were (100, 40,000 USD), (25, 85 years), (0, 100%) and (0, 100%), respectively. The indicator functions f, which determine the indicators A according to equation (9.5), is the identity function, except for $i = 1$: For gross domestic product per capita, the natural logarithm is taken instead. Hence, in (9.5) we have the respective, different indicator functions

$$f_1(x_1) = \ln x_1; \quad f_2(x_2) = x_2, \quad f_3(x_3) = x_3, \quad f_4(x_4) = x_4$$

$$(9.7)$$

(The identity function is concave; the natural logarithm is strictly concave.). The weights $1/k$ in equation (9.6) are $1/3$ (gross domestic product per capita), $1/3$ (life expectancy), $2/9$ (literacy), and $1/9$ (gross enrollment ratio), to reflect that the last two attributes ($i = 3$ and 4) represent one of the three dimensions, namely education. This completes the description of the so-called old HDI.

The 2010 HDI introduced three modifications. First, there were two measurement refinements, the gross domestic product was replaced by gross national income (GNI), and literacy and gross enrollment ratio by mean years of schooling and expected years of schooling. Second, the lower and upper bounds were fine tuned. Third, the arithmetic average (9.6) was replaced by a geometric average, $\prod_{i=1}^{k} a_i^{1/k}$. However, since the main purpose of the HDI is ranking across countries, we may just as well take a monotonic transformation, say the natural logarithm. In other words, the main change in the 2010 revision amounts to taking the natural logarithm of the indicator values a_i.

The most recent HDI ranking can be found in the 2020 Human Development Report by the United Nations Development Programme (2020, p. 343 and further) and is reproduced in the Appendix. The dimensions a_1, a_2, a_3 and a_4 are listed at the top, preceded by the column with HDI scores and followed by the column with just the traditional GNI. The countries are ranked by HDI score. The table also presents the difference in rankings by HDI value and GNI per capita (see United Nations Development Programme (2020, p. 338) — the column heading on p. 343 of that publication is wrong and has been corrected in the Appendix). A column with the HDI rank of the preceding year is added to see the trends. Norway continued to top the HDI list. The United Arab Emirates rank one higher than Norway by GNI per capita, but far lower by HDI. The difference in rankings by HDI value and GNI per capita is 7 for Norway and -24 for the United Arab Emirates. The second place has been captured by Ireland, from Switzerland, though their rankings are equal at the level of reported digits.

Let us give the broad measures of well-being a place in our framework of strictly economic consumer's well-being, the consumer's index. Following McFadden (2014), collect the values of the non-market goods and the environmental indicators in a vector z. The consumer chooses a commodity bundle x and faces circumstances z. The correspondence with the HDI is that the first HDI variable, gross national income x_1, corresponds with bundle x and income m, while the other HDI variables correspond with vector z. Anyway, the problem of the consumer (2.1) is replaced by $\max_x U(x, z) : px \leq m$ and now has solution $x = D(p, z, m)$ with utility $u = U(D(p, z, m))$. The expenditure function turns the solution to $\min_x px : U(x, z) \geq u$ and is denoted by $e(p, z, u)$. Let the price vector change from p to p', the budget from m to m', and the non-economic indicators from z to z'. As a result, utility u changes to u'. Standard of living measures (3.5) and (3.6) are now broadened as follows.

Definition: The *broad measure of the equivalent variation-based standard of living* equals $e(p, z, u') - e(p, z, u)$.

Definition: The *broad measure of the compensating variation-based standard of living* equals $e(p', z', u') - e(p', z', u)$.

The broad measures can be written as Hicksian integrals of compensated demand functions, using Shephard's lemma (Chapter 2). To reveal the integrals, separate the price and income effects in the broad measures by using the identities $e(p, z, u) = m$ and $e(p', z', u') = m'$ (assuming local nonsatiation). Thus, the broad measure of the equivalent variation-based standard of living equals $e(p, z, u') - e(p', z', u') + m' - m = \Delta m - E$, where $E = e(p', z', u') - e(p, z, u')$ is the equivalent variation, (3.1), complicated, however, by a simultaneous change in the non-economic indicators, from z to z'. The equivalent variation E equals the line integral $\int_{(p,z)}^{(p',z')} \left(\frac{\partial e(p'', z'', u')}{\partial p} \frac{\partial e(p'', z'', u')}{\partial z} \right) \left(\frac{dp''}{dz''} \right)$, which is, by Shephard's lemma (Chapter 2), $\int_{(p,z)}^{(p',z')} \left(D^c(p'', z'', u') \frac{\partial e(p'', z'', u')}{\partial z} \right) \left(\frac{dp''}{dz''} \right)$. This is path independent simply because $e(p'', z'', u')$ is a potential function. Likewise, the broad measure of the compensating variation-based standard of living equals $m' - m + e(p, z, u) - e(p', z', u) = \Delta m - C$, where $C = e(p', z', u) - e(p, z, u)$ is the compensating variation, (3.2), complicated, however, by a simultaneous change in the non-economic indicators, from z to z'. The compensating variation C equals the line integral $\int_{(p,z)}^{(p',z')} \left(\frac{\partial e(p'', z'', u)}{\partial p} \frac{\partial e(p'', z'', u)}{\partial z} \right) \left(\frac{dp''}{dz''} \right)$, which is, by Shephard's lemma (Chapter 2), $\int_{(p,z)}^{(p',z')} \left(D^c(p'', z'', u) \frac{\partial e(p'', z'', u)}{\partial z} \right) \left(\frac{dp''}{dz''} \right)$. This is path independent simply because $e(p'', z'', u)$ is a potential function. Both measures inherit the failure to track utility from their non-broadened counterparts and the question is if this can be fixed by broadening the consumer's index, $CI = \int_{(p,m)}^{(p',m')} \frac{dm'' - D(p'', m'')dp''}{m''}$. The necessary and sufficient condition for path independence of line integral CI is quasihomotheticity of demand. A successful broadening of CI should at least work in the special case that demand is homothetic, $D(p, m) = mD(p, 1)$. Then $CI = \ln(m'/m) - \int_p^{p'} D(p'', 1)dp''$ (8.7). Demand is broadened to $D(p, z, m)$ and hence the CI integrand to $D(p, z, 1)$. Broad CI becomes $\ln(m'/m) - \int_{(p,z)}^{(p',z')} [D(p'', z'', 1)dp'' + \xi(p'', z'', 1)dz'']$. Here, ξ is the row vector of *marginal monetary valuations of the non-economic indicators*. The applied broad measures feature indicators which are constant and price independent, so that function ξ reduces to a constant row vector of weights for the various non-economic components and, therefore, broad CI reduces to

$$\text{broad } CI = \ln(m'/m) - \int_{(p,z)}^{(p',z')} [D(p'', z'', 1)dp'' + \xi dz'']$$

$$(9.8)$$

To be well-defined the combined price (p) nonprice (z) effect must be path independent. Recall that a line integral of the form $\int_x^{x'} h(x'')dx''$ is path independent (if and) only if the matrix of partial derivatives of h is symmetric. In the broad consumer's index, the variable is the vector of price and non-price indices, $x = (p, z)$, and the function is $h(p, z) = (D(p, z, 1)\xi)$. Symmetry of the matrix of partial derivatives means that the demand for economic goods must be independent of the non-economic indicators. As a result, broad consumer's index (9.8) reduces to

$$\ln(m'/m) - \int_p^{p'} D(p'', 1, 1)dp'' + \xi(z' - z) \qquad (9.9)$$

Equation (9.9) is the consumer's index (8.7) augmented with a linear term to incorporate the non-economic indicators. Of course, quite a job must be done to estimate the marginal monetary valuations of the non-economic indicators. However, we have done so for the important case of CO_2 emissions using a general equilibrium framework that deals with consumer preferences; I refer to ten Raa and Shestalova (2015).

The consumer's index is consumer's surplus normalized by income hence dimensionless, hence, the non-economic add-on must also be dimensionless. However, there is an asymmetry. The economic demand parameters can be estimated if there are sufficiently many observations. In fact, even the various consumer well-being measures can be estimated, because the underlying consumer preferences can be recovered from demand, assuming consumers choose according to their own preferences (Hurwicz and Uzawa, 1971). This recoverability does not hold for the non-economic component of consumer well-being. The weights of the non-economic indicators are hard to estimate. McFadden (2014) discusses contemporary attempts to go outside the neoclassical model to measure such effects by either 'making a market' via incentive-compatible mechanisms for eliciting values, or by utilizing biometric measures of hedonic state.

At the more macro-economic level, there is a similarity between the human development index and the broad consumer's index. The HDI features linear indicator functions for the non-economic indicators and the logarithmic indicator function for the economic indicator. Equation (9.7) shows the difference and thus feeds HDI (9.6) via indicators (9.5). Broad *CI* (9.9) features three terms, logarithmic income, linear non-economic contributions, and income normalized consumer's surplus. The HDI catches the first two components and misses the latter, simply because of its neglect of consumer's preferences.

Chapter 10

Conclusion

Consumer's surplus measures the difference between the willingness to pay, as reflected by the (inverse) demand function, and the price, and integrates between two prices, the base price and the current price. Thus, it is the area between the demand curve and the price line. When price goes up, the area under the demand curve between the base price and the current price measures the loss of consumer's surplus. This simplicity makes the concept of consumer's surplus a popular measure of consumer economic well-being. However, it has been discredited by economic theorists. They have two objections. The first objection is a definitional issue. The variation of consumer's surplus is the integral of demand between two prices. When there are several goods, consumer's surplus is the integral of demand between two price vectors. However, the integral depends on the path of integration, and that is considered bad, rendering the concept ill-defined. The second, related objection is that the variation of consumer's surplus merely approximates two other measures, namely the equivalent variation and the compensating variation, while theorists argue there is no need to approximate. If sufficient information is available, one can go for the real thing, e.g., the equivalent and compensating variations.

However, in this book I have resurrected consumer's surplus. My point of departure has been to check if a measure of consumer economic well-being tracks utility. Does a measure go up or down when utility goes up or down? I presented a useful test. A well-being index tracks utility only if it passes a homogeneity test. The equivalent variation, the compensating variation, and the variation of consumer's surplus all fail the test. However, if consumer's surplus is normalized by income, it passes the test and tracks utility, at least when utility is homothetic, meaning that the proportions of demand remain the same when income grows but prices are constant. In this sense, modified consumer's surplus beats the equivalent and compensating variations. This slight modification of consumer's surplus, the normalization by income, defines the consumer's index.

Of course, there are two momentous restrictions. First, the reasoning is sound for individual demands. And second, homotheticity presumes there are no income effects. Of course, it remains of interest that consumer's surplus beats the so-called 'exact' measures of equivalent and compensating variations under these restrictions. If they would be superior, they should certainly be superior for individual demand functions with no income effects. But what about market demands and what about income effects? I have explored these extensions in detail and shown that extensions are possible. The two issues, the extension to market demands and the incorporation of income effects, have been addressed in a unified way, drawing on the microeconomic literature of demand aggregation. First and foremost, the absence of income effects — that is the assumption that Engel curves are straight and radiate from the origin of the commodity space — can be relaxed to straight Engel curves radiating not from the origin but from an alternative point or even from a so-called subsistence surface. This is the key element of a perfect aggregation condition, by which market demand can be thought to be generated by a representative consumer. The nice feature of this generalization is that any Engel curve can be approximated locally this way. Second, there is a further modification of the analysis where the demand relations are not linear but loglinear, accommodating nonlinear Engel curves. This analysis builds on the demand literature and admits a variant of consumer's surplus that does the job of tracking utility. Moreover, non-economic indices, such as health and environmental indicators, can be accommodated by the consumer's index.

The motivation of this study was a critical analysis of the claim that the equivalent variation and the compensating variation are exact measures of consumer well-being, while consumer's surplus is only an approximation. The result is quite the opposite. For the simple case of homothetic demand, income normalized consumer's surplus, the consumer's index for short, is the exact measure of utility, while the two variations are not. And if the equivalent and compensating variations are inferior in the simple, homothetic case, there is no hope they are superior in other, more complicated situations. However, an issue is if the consumer's index is also applicable to non-homothetic demands. Well, the answer is a ringing yes for quasi-homothetic demands (with parallel linear Engel curves) and, very pleasing, their associated aggregate demand. There remains the issue if the consumer's index is extendable to demands with nonlinear Engel curves, and the answer is still affirmative. The measures of consumer well-being have been shaken up.

Appendix: Human Development Index and Its Components

Source: 2020 Human Development Report, United Nations Development Programme

HDI RANK	Human Development Index (HDI) Value 2019	Life expectancy at birth (years) 2019	Expected years of schooling (years) 2019a	Mean years of schooling (years) 2019a	Gross national income (GNI) per capita (2017 PPP $) 2019	HDI rank minus GNI per capita rank 2019	HDI rank 2018
Very high human development							
1 Norway	0.957	82.4	18.1[b]	12.9	66,494	7	1
2 Ireland	0.955	82.3	18.7[b]	12.7	68,371	4	3
2 Switzerland	0.955	83.8	16.3	13.4	69,394	3	2
4 Hong Kong, China (SAR)	0.949	84.9	16.9	12.3	62,985	7	4
4 Iceland	0.949	83.0	19.1[b]	12.8[c]	54,682	14	4
6 Germany	0.947	81.3	17.0	14.2	55,314	11	4
7 Sweden	0.945	82.8	19.5[b]	12.5	54,508	12	7
8 Australia	0.944	83.4	22.0[b]	12.7[c]	48,085	15	7
8 Netherlands	0.944	82.3	18.5[b]	12.4	57,707	6	9
10 Denmark	0.940	80.9	18.9[b]	12.6[c]	58,662	2	10
11 Finland	0.938	81.9	19.4[b]	12.8	48,511	11	11
11 Singapore	0.938	83.6	16.4	11.6	88,155[d]	−8	12
13 United Kingdom	0.932	81.3	17.5	13.2	46,071	13	14
14 Belgium	0.931	81.6	19.8[b]	12.1[e]	52,085	6	13
14 New Zealand	0.931	82.3	18.8[b]	12.8[c]	40,799	18	14
16 Canada	0.929	82.4	16.2	13.4[c]	48,527	5	14
17 United States	0.926	78.9	16.3	13.4	63,826	−7	17
18 Austria	0.922	81.5	16.1	12.5[c]	56,197	−3	18
19 Israel	0.919	83.0	16.2	13.0	40,187	14	21
19 Japan	0.919	84.6	15.2	12.9[f]	42,932	9	20
19 Liechtenstein	0.919	80.7[g]	14.9	12.5[h]	131,032[d,i]	−18	19
22 Slovenia	0.917	81.3	17.6	12.7	38,080	15	24
23 Korea (Republic of)	0.916	83.0	16.5	12.2	43,044	4	22
23 Luxembourg	0.916	82.3	14.3	12.3[e]	72,712	−19	23

HDI RANK		Human Development Index (HDI)	Life expectancy at birth	Expected years of schooling	Mean years of schooling	Gross national income (GNI) per capita	HDI rank minus GNI per capita rank		HDI rank
		Value	(years)	(years)	(years)	(2017 PPP $)			
		2019	2019	2019[a]	2019[a]	2019	2019	2018	2018
25	Spain	0.904	83.6	17.6	10.3	40,975	6		25
26	France	0.901	82.7	15.6	11.5	47,173	−1		26
27	Czechia	0.900	79.4	16.8	12.7[c]	38,109	9		26
28	Malta	0.895	82.5	16.1	11.3	39,555	6		28
29	Estonia	0.892	78.8	16.0	13.1[c]	36,019	9		30
29	Italy	0.892	83.5	16.1	10.4[j]	42,776	0		29
31	United Arab Emirates	0.890	78.0	14.3	12.1	67,462	−24		30
32	Greece	0.888	82.2	17.9	10.6	30,155	14		33
33	Cyprus	0.887	81.0	15.2	12.2	38,207	2		32
34	Lithuania	0.882	75.9	16.6	13.1	35,799	5		35
34	Poland	0.880	78.7	16.3	12.5[e]	31,623	8		34
36	Andorra	0.868	81.9[g]	13.3[k]	10.5	56,000[l]	−20		36
37	Latvia	0.866	75.3	16.2	13.0[c]	30,282	8		37
38	Portugal	0.864	82.1	16.5	9.3	33,967	2		38
39	Slovakia	0.860	77.5	14.5	12.7[c]	32,113	3		39
40	Hungary	0.854	76.9	15.2	12.0	31,329	4		42
40	Saudi Arabia	0.854	75.1	16.1	10.2	47,495	−16		40
42	Bahrain	0.852	77.3	16.3	9.5	42,522	−12		41
43	Chile	0.851	80.2	16.4	10.6	23,261	16		43
43	Croatia	0.851	78.5	15.2	11.4[e]	28,070	6		44
45	Qatar	0.848	80.2	12.0	9.7	92,418[d]	−43		45
46	Argentina	0.845	76.7	17.7	10.9[c]	21,190	16		46
47	Brunei Darussalam	0.838	75.9	14.3	9.1[f]	63,965	−38		47
48	Montenegro	0.829	76.9	15.0	11.6[m]	21,399	13		48

(Continued)

(*Continued*)

HDI RANK	Human Development Index (HDI) Value 2019	Life expectancy at birth (years) 2019	Expected years of schooling (years) 2019[a]	Mean years of schooling (years) 2019[a]	Gross national income (GNI) per capita (2017 PPP $) 2019	HDI rank minus GNI per capita rank 2019	HDI rank 2018
49 Romania	0.828	76.1	14.3	11.1	29,497	−1	49
50 Palau	0.826	73.9[g]	15.8[j]	12.5[j]	19,317	15	52
51 Kazakhstan	0.825	73.6	15.6	11.9[j]	22,857	9	53
52 Russian Federation	0.824	72.6	15.0	12.2[j]	26,157	2	49
53 Belarus	0.823	74.8	15.4	12.3[m]	18,546	14	49
54 Turkey	0.820	77.7	16.6[c]	8.1	27,701	−4	54
55 Uruguay	0.817	77.9	16.8	8.9	20,064	9	56
56 Bulgaria	0.816	75.1	14.4	11.4	23,325	2	55
57 Panama	0.815	78.5	12.9	10.2[f]	29,558	−10	58
58 Bahamas	0.814	73.9	12.9[n]	11.4[j]	33,747	−17	58
58 Barbados	0.814	79.2	15.4	10.6[o]	14,936	20	60
60 Oman	0.813	77.9	14.2	9.7[j]	25,944	−5	56
61 Georgia	0.812	73.8	15.3	13.1	14,429	22	63
62 Costa Rica	0.810	80.3	15.7	8.7	18,486	6	61
62 Malaysia	0.810	76.2	13.7	10.4	27,534	−11	63
64 Kuwait	0.806	75.5	14.2	7.3	58,590	−51	62
64 Serbia	0.806	76.0	14.7	11.2	17,192	8	65
66 Mauritius	0.804	75.0	15.1	9.5[f]	25,266	−10	66
High human development							
67 Seychelles	0.796	73.4	14.1	10.0[k]	26,903	−15	69
67 Trinidad and Tobago	0.796	73.5	13.0[j]	11.0[f]	26,231	−14	67
69 Albania	0.795	78.6	14.7	10.1[p]	13,998	18	68
70 Cuba	0.783	78.8	14.3	11.8[j]	8,621[q]	45	71

HDI RANK		Human Development Index (HDI)	Life expectancy at birth	Expected years of schooling	Mean years of schooling	Gross national income (GNI) per capita	HDI rank minus GNI per capita rank	HDI rank
		Value	(years)	(years)	(years)	(2017 PPP $)		
		2019	2019	2019a	2019a	2019	2019	2018
70	Iran (Islamic Republic of)	0.783	76.7	14.8	10.3	12,447	26	70
72	Sri Lanka	0.782	77.0	14.1	10.6	12,707	23	73
73	Bosnia and Herzegovina	0.780	77.4	13.8k	9.8	14,872	7	76
74	Grenada	0.779	72.4	16.9	9.0n	15,641	3	74
74	Mexico	0.779	75.1	14.8	8.8	19,160	−8	76
74	Saint Kitts and Nevis	0.779	74.8g	13.8j	8.7n	25,038	−17	75
74	Ukraine	0.779	72.1	15.1j	11.4o	13,216	19	78
78	Antigua and Barbuda	0.778	77.0	12.8j	9.3k	20,895	−15	80
79	Peru	0.777	76.7	15.0	9.7	12,252	19	78
79	Thailand	0.777	77.2	15.0j	7.9	17,781	−10	80
81	Armenia	0.776	75.1	13.1	11.3	13,894	9	72
82	North Macedonia	0.774	75.8	13.6	9.8m	15,865	−7	82
83	Colombia	0.767	77.3	14.4	8.5	14,257	3	83
84	Brazil	0.765	75.9	15.4	8.0	14,263	1	84
85	China	0.761	76.9	14.0j	8.1f	16,057	−11	87
86	Ecuador	0.759	77.0	14.6j	8.9	11,044	19	84
86	Saint Lucia	0.759	76.2	14.0j	8.5j	14,616	−4	86
88	Azerbaijan	0.756	73.0	12.9j	10.6	13,784	3	88
88	Dominican Republic	0.756	74.1	14.2	8.1j	17,591	−18	89
90	Moldova (Republic of)	0.750	71.9	11.5	11.7	13,664	2	91
91	Algeria	0.748	76.9	14.6	8.0m	11,174	13	91
92	Lebanon	0.744	78.9	11.3	8.7n	14,655	−11	90
93	Fiji	0.743	67.4	14.4n	10.9	13,009	1	93
94	Dominica	0.742	78.2g	13.0p	8.1k	11,884	7	94
95	Maldives	0.740	78.9	12.2p	7.0p	17,417	−24	98

(Continued)

(Continued)

HDI RANK	Human Development Index (HDI) Value 2019	Life expectancy at birth (years) 2019	Expected years of schooling (years) 2019[a]	Mean years of schooling (years) 2019[a]	Gross national income (GNI) per capita (2017 PPP $) 2019	HDI rank minus GNI per capita rank 2019	HDI rank 2018
95 Tunisia	0.740	76.7	15.1	7.2	10,414	14	94
97 Saint Vincent and the Grenadines	0.738	72.5	14.1^j	8.8^j	12,378	0	96
97 Suriname	0.738	71.7	13.2	9.3^m	14,324	−13	98
99 Mongolia	0.737	69.9	14.2^j	10.3^m	10,839	7	97
100 Botswana	0.735	69.6	12.8^j	9.6^o	16,437	−27	102
101 Jamaica	0.734	74.5	13.1^j	9.7^j	9,319	13	98
102 Jordan	0.729	74.5	11.4^p	10.5^f	9,858	8	103
103 Paraguay	0.728	74.3	12.7^m	8.5	12,224	−4	104
104 Tonga	0.725	70.9	14.4^j	11.2^f	6,365	25	105
105 Libya	0.724	72.9	12.9^n	7.6^o	15,688	−29	106
106 Uzbekistan	0.720	71.7	12.1	11.8	7,142	17	107
107 Bolivia (Plurinational State of)	0.718	71.5	14.2^r	9.0	8,554	9	108
107 Indonesia	0.718	71.7	13.6	8.2	11,459	−4	110
107 Philippines	0.718	71.2	13.1	9.4	9,778	4	111
110 Belize	0.716	74.6	13.1	9.9^m	6,382	18	108
111 Samoa	0.715	73.3	12.7^j	10.8	6,309	19	113
111 Turkmenistan	0.715	68.2	11.2^j	10.3^m	14,909	−32	112
113 Venezuela (Bolivarian Republic of)	0.711	72.1	12.8^j	10.3	7,045^s	11	101
114 South Africa	0.709	64.1	13.8	10.2	12,129	−14	115
115 Palestine, State of	0.708	74.1	13.4	9.2	6,417	12	114
116 Egypt	0.707	72.0	13.3	7.4^f	11,466	−14	117

HDI RANK	Human Development Index (HDI) Value 2019	Life expectancy at birth (years) 2019	Expected years of schooling (years) 2019[a]	Mean years of schooling (years) 2019[a]	Gross national income (GNI) per capita (2017 PPP \$) 2019	HDI rank minus GNI per capita rank 2019	HDI rank 2018
117 Marshall Islands	0.704	74.1[g]	12.4[n]	10.9[j]	5,039	21	116
117 Viet Nam	0.704	75.4	12.7[j]	8.3[f]	7,433	3	118
119 Gabon	0.703	66.5	13.0[n]	8.7[f]	13,930	−30	119
Medium human development							
120 Kyrgyzstan	0.697	71.5	13.0	11.1[m]	4,864	23	120
121 Morocco	0.686	76.7	13.7	5.6[f]	7,368	1	121
122 Guyana	0.682	69.9	11.4[j]	8.5[m]	9,455	−10	121
123 Iraq	0.674	70.6	11.3[m]	7.3[j]	10,801	−16	123
124 El Salvador	0.673	73.3	11.7	6.9	8,359	−6	124
125 Tajikistan	0.668	71.1	11.7[j]	10.7[p]	3,954	25	126
126 Cabo Verde	0.665	73.0	12.7	6.3[j]	7,019	−1	125
127 Guatemala	0.663	74.3	10.8	6.6	8,494	−10	128
128 Nicaragua	0.660	74.5	12.3[r]	6.9[f]	5,284	6	127
129 Bhutan	0.654	71.8	13.0	4.1	10,746	−21	131
130 Namibia	0.646	63.7	12.6[j]	7.0[f]	9,357	−17	129
131 India	0.645	69.7	12.2	6.5[j]	6,681	−5	130
132 Honduras	0.634	75.3	10.1	6.6	5,308	1	132
133 Bangladesh	0.632	72.6	11.6	6.2	4,976	7	134
134 Kiribati	0.630	68.4	11.8[m]	8.0[m]	4,260	12	133
135 Sao Tome and Principe	0.625	70.4	12.7[j]	6.4[j]	3,952	16	135
136 Micronesia (Federated States of)	0.620	67.9	11.5[k]	7.8[n]	3,983	13	136
137 Lao People's Democratic Republic	0.613	67.9	11.0	5.3[f]	7,413	−16	137
138 Eswatini (Kingdom of)	0.611	60.2	11.8[j]	6.9[m]	7,919	−19	139

(Continued)

(*Continued*)

HDI RANK	Human Development Index (HDI) Value 2019	Life expectancy at birth (years) 2019	Expected years of schooling (years) 2019[a]	Mean years of schooling (years) 2019[a]	Gross national income (GNI) per capita (2017 PPP $) 2019	HDI rank minus GNI per capita rank 2019	HDI rank 2018
138 Ghana	0.611	64.1	11.5	7.3[f]	5,269	−3	138
140 Vanuatu	0.609	70.5	11.7[n]	7.1	3,105	20	140
141 Timor-Leste	0.606	69.5	12.6[j]	4.8[p]	4,440	3	141
142 Nepal	0.602	70.8	12.8	5.0[f]	3,457	13	143
143 Kenya	0.601	66.7	11.3[p]	6.6[f]	4,244	5	141
144 Cambodia	0.594	69.8	11.5[p]	5.0[f]	4,246	3	144
145 Equatorial Guinea	0.592	58.7	9.7[n]	5.9[k]	13,944	−57	145
146 Zambia	0.584	63.9	11.5[p]	7.2[p]	3,326	10	145
147 Myanmar	0.583	67.1	10.7	5.0[p]	4,961	−6	148
148 Angola	0.581	61.2	11.8[p]	5.2[p]	6,104	−17	145
149 Congo	0.574	64.6	11.7[n]	6.5[o]	2,879	13	149
150 Zimbabwe	0.571	61.5	11.0[m]	8.5	2,666	14	150
151 Solomon Islands	0.567	73.0	10.2[j]	5.7[m]	2,253	17	151
151 Syrian Arab Republic	0.567	72.7	8.9[j]	5.1[n]	3,613[t]	2	152
153 Cameroon	0.563	59.3	12.1	6.3[m]	3,581	1	153
154 Pakistan	0.557	67.3	8.3	5.2	5,005	−15	154
155 Papua New Guinea	0.555	64.5	10.2[p]	4.7[f]	4,301	−10	156
156 Comoros	0.554	64.3	11.2	5.1[n]	3,099	5	154
Low human development							
157 Mauritania	0.546	64.9	8.6	4.7[f]	5,135	−21	157
158 Benin	0.545	61.8	12.6	3.8[p]	3,254	0	158
159 Uganda	0.544	63.4	11.4[p]	6.2[p]	2,123	15	160
160 Rwanda	0.543	69.0	11.2	4.4[j]	2,155	12	159

HDI RANK	Human Development Index (HDI) Value 2019	Life expectancy at birth (years) 2019	Expected years of schooling (years) 2019[a]	Mean years of schooling (years) 2019[a]	Gross national income (GNI) per capita (2017 PPP $) 2019	HDI rank minus GNI per capita rank 2019	HDI rank 2018
161 Nigeria	0.539	54.7	10.0[p]	6.7[p]	4,910	−19	161
162 Côte d'Ivoire	0.538	57.8	10.0	5.3[f]	5,069	−25	161
163 Tanzania (United Republic of)	0.529	65.5	8.1	6.1[f]	2,600	2	164
164 Madagascar	0.528	67.0	10.2	6.1[n]	1,596	16	163
165 Lesotho	0.527	54.3	11.3[j]	6.5[m]	3,151	−6	165
166 Djibouti	0.524	67.1	6.8[j]	4.1[n]	5,689	−34	166
167 Togo	0.515	61.0	12.7	4.9[m]	1,602	12	168
168 Senegal	0.512	67.9	8.6	3.2[j]	3,309	−11	167
169 Afghanistan	0.511	64.8	10.2	3.9[f]	2,229	0	169
170 Haiti	0.510	64.0	9.7[j]	5.6[p]	1,709	7	170
170 Sudan	0.510	65.3	7.9[j]	3.8[f]	3,829	−18	171
172 Gambia	0.496	62.1	9.9[p]	3.9[m]	2,168	−1	172
173 Ethiopia	0.485	66.6	8.8[j]	2.9[p]	2,207	−3	174
174 Malawi	0.483	64.3	11.2[j]	4.7[f]	1,035	13	174
175 Congo (Democratic Republic of the)	0.480	60.7	9.7[j]	6.8	1,063	11	174
175 Guinea-Bissau	0.480	58.3	10.6[m]	3.6[m]	1,996	1	178
175 Liberia	0.480	64.1	9.6[n]	4.8[f]	1,258	8	173
178 Guinea	0.477	61.6	9.4[m,p]	2.8[p]	2,405	−12	177
179 Yemen	0.470	66.1	8.8[j]	3.2[f]	1,594[t]	2	179

(Continued)

(*Continued*)

HDI RANK	Human Development Index (HDI) Value 2019	Life expectancy at birth (years) 2019	Expected years of schooling (years) 2019[a]	Mean years of schooling (years) 2019[a]	Gross national income (GNI) per capita (2017 PPP \$) 2019	HDI rank minus GNI per capita rank 2019	HDI rank 2018
180 Eritrea	0.459	66.3	5.0^j	3.9^n	2,793^u	−17	180
181 Mozambique	0.456	60.9	10.0	3.5^j	1,250	3	181
182 Burkina Faso	0.452	61.6	9.3	1.6^p	2,133	−9	183
182 Sierra Leone	0.452	54.7	10.2^j	3.7^f	1,668	−4	182
184 Mali	0.434	59.3	7.5	2.4^m	2,269	−17	184
185 Burundi	0.433	61.6	11.1	3.3^p	754	4	184
185 South Sudan	0.433	57.9	5.3^n	4.8^n	2,003^u	−10	186
187 Chad	0.398	54.2	7.3	2.5^p	1,555	−5	187
188 Central African Republic	0.397	53.3	7.6^j	4.3^f	993	0	188
189 Niger	0.394	62.4	6.5	2.1^j	1,201	−4	189
Other countries or territories							
Korea (Democratic People's Rep. of)	—	72.3	10.8^j	—	—	—	—
Monaco	—	—	—	—	—	—	—
Nauru	—	—	11.2^j	—	16,237	—	—
San Marino	—	—	13.0	—	—	—	—
Somalia	—	57.4	—	—	—	—	—
Tuvalu	—	—	12.3^j	—	6,132	—	—
Human development groups							
Very high human development	0.898	79.6	16.3	12.2	44,566	—	
High human development	0.753	75.3	14.0	8.4	14,255	—	
Medium human development	0.631	69.3	11.5	6.3	6,153	—	

HDI RANK	Human Development Index (HDI) Value 2019	Life expectancy at birth (years) 2019	Expected years of schooling (years) 2019ᵃ	Mean years of schooling (years) 2019ᵃ	Gross national income (GNI) per capita (2017 PPP $) 2019	HDI rank minus GNI per capita rank 2019	HDI rank 2018
Low human development	0.513	61.4	9.4	4.9	2,745	—	—
Developing countries	0.689	71.3	12.2	7.5	10,583	—	—
Regions							
Arab States	0.705	72.1	12.1	7.3	14,869	—	—
East Asia and the Pacific	0.747	75.4	13.6	8.1	14,710	—	—
Europe and Central Asia	0.791	74.4	14.7	10.4	17,939	—	—
Latin America and the Caribbean	0.766	75.6	14.6	8.7	14,812	—	—
South Asia	0.641	69.9	11.7	6.5	6,532	—	—
Sub-Saharan Africa	0.547	61.5	10.1	5.8	3,686	—	—
Least developed countries	0.538	65.3	9.9	4.9	2,935	—	—
Small island developing states	0.728	72.0	12.3	8.7	16,825	—	—
Organisation for Economic Co-operation and Development	0.900	80.4	16.3	12.0	44,967	—	—
World	**0.737**	**72.8**	**12.7**	**8.5**	**16,734**	—	—

Source: 2020 Human Development Report, United Nations Development Programme, New York (2020)

Definitions

Human Development Index (HDI): A composite index measuring average achievement in three basic dimensions of human development — a long and healthy life, knowledge and a decent standard of living. See *Technical note 1* at http://hdr.undp.org/sites/default/files/hdr2020_technical_notes.pdf for details on how the HDI is calculated.

Life expectancy at birth: Number of years a newborn infant could expect to live if prevailing patterns of age-specific mortality rates at the time of birth stay the same throughout the infant's life.

Expected years of schooling: Number of years of schooling that a child of school entrance age can expect to receive if prevailing patterns of age-specific enrolment rates persist throughout the child's life.

Mean years of schooling: Average number of years of education received by people ages 25 and older, converted from education attainment levels using official durations of each level.

Gross national income (GNI) per capita: Aggregate income of an economy generated by its production and its ownership of factors of production, less the incomes paid for the use of factors of production owned by the rest of the world, converted to international dollars using PPP rates, divided by midyear population.

GNI per capita rank minus HDI rank: Difference in ranking by GNI per capita and by HDI value. A negative value means that the country is better ranked by GNI than by HDI value.

HDI rank for 2018: Ranking by HDI value for 2018, calculated using the same most recently revised data available in 2020 that were used to calculate HDI values for 2019.

Sources:

Columns 1 and 7: HDRO calculations based on data from UNDESA (2019), UNESCO Institute for Statistics (2020), United Nations Statistics Division (2020), World Bank (2020), Barro and Lee (2018) and IMF (2020).

Column 2: UNDESA (2019).

Column 3: UNESCO Institute for Statistics (2020), ICF Macro Demographic and Health Surveys, UNICEF Multiple Indicator Cluster Surveys and OECD (2019).

Column 4: UNESCO Institute for Statistics (2020), Barro and Lee (2018), ICF Macro Demographic and Health Surveys, UNICEF Multiple Indicator Cluster Surveys and OECD (2019).

Column 5: World Bank (2020), IMF (2020) and United Nations Statistics Division (2020).

Column 6: Calculated based on data in columns 1 and 5.

References

S. P. Anderson, A. de Palma, and J.-F. Thisse, *Discrete Choice Theory of Product Differentiation*, MIT Press, Cambridge, MA, (1992).

R. J. Barro and J.-W. Lee, *Dataset of Educational Attainment*, Revision (June 2018). www.barrolee.com. Accessed 20 July 2020.

J.-P. Benassy, "Taste for Variety and Optimum Production Patterns in Monopolistic Competition," *Economics Letters* 52, 41–7 (1996).

C. Blackorby, R. Boyce, and R. R. Russell, "Estimation of Demand Systems Generated by the Gorman Polar Form; A Generalization of the S-branch Utility Tree," *Econometrica* 46, 2, 345–63 (1978).

N. Bruce, "A Note on Consumer's Surplus, the Divisia Index, and the Measurement of Welfare Changes," *Econometrica* 45, 4, 1033–8 (1977).

S. R. Chakravarty, "A Generalized Human Development Index," *Review of Development Economics* 7, 1, 99–114 (2003).

L. R. Christensen, D. W. Jorgenson, and L. J. Lau, "Transcendental Logarithmic Utility Functions," *American Economic Review* 65, 3, 367–83 (1975).

A. Deaton, "Demand Analysis," in Z. Griliches and M. D. Intriligator (eds.): *Handbook of Econometrics* 3, Elsevier, Amsterdam, 30 (1986).

A. Deaton, "Measuring and Understanding Behavior, Welfare, and Poverty," *American Economic Review* 106, 6, 1221–43 (2016).

A. Deaton and J. Muellbauer, "An Almost Ideal Demand System," *American Economic Review* 70, 3, 312–26 (1980).

G. Debreu, "The Coefficient of Resource Utilization," *Econometrica* 19, 3, 273–92 (1951).

F. Divisia, "L'Indice Monétaire et la Théorie de la Monnaie," *Revue d'Économie Politique* 39, 4, 842–61 (1925).

A. K. Dixit and J. E. Stiglitz, "Monopolistic Competition and Optimum Product Diversity," *American Economic Review* 67, 3, 297–308 (1977).

R. C. Geary, "A Note on "A Constant-Utility Index of the Cost of Living," *Review of Economic Studies* 18, 1, 65–6 (1950).

W. M. Gorman, "Community Preference Fields," *Econometrica* 21, 1, 63–80 (1953).

W. M. Gorman, "Separable Utility and Aggregation," *Econometrica* 27, 3, 469–81 (1959).

W. M. Gorman, "On a Class of Preference Fields," *Metroeconomica* 13, 2, 53–6 (1961).

W. M. Gorman, "Tricks with Utility Functions," in M. J. Artis and A. R. Nobay (eds.): *Essays in Economic Analysis*, Cambridge University Press, Cambridge, 211–43 (1976).

V. Halsmayer, "Artifacts in the Contemporary History of Economics," in T. Düppe and E. R. Weintraub (eds.): *A Contemporary Historiography of Economics*, Routledge, Abingdon and NewYork, 157–76 (2019).

J. A. Hausman, "Exact Consumer's Surplus and Deadweight Loss," *American Economic Review* 71, 4, 662–76 (1981).

J. R. Hicks, "Consumers' Surplus and Index-Numbers," *Review of Economic Studies* 9, 2, 126–37 (1942).

P. Honohan and J. P. Neary, "W. M. Gorman (1923–2003)," *Economic and Social Review* 34, 2, 195–209 (2003).

L. Hurwicz and H. Uzawa, "On the Integrability of Demand Functions," in J. S. Chipman, L. Hurwicz, M. K. Richter, and H. F. Sonnenschein (eds.): *Preferences, Utility and Demand*, Harcourt, Brace, Jovanovich, New York, 114–48 (1971).

ICF Macro, *Demographic and Health Surveys*. www.measuredhs.com. Accessed 15 July 2020.

International Monetary Fund (IMF), *World Economic Outlook Database*, Washington, DC (2020). www.imf.org/external/pubs/ft/weo/2020/01/weodata/index.aspx. Accessed 15 July 2020.

D. W. Jorgenson, "Aggregate Consumer Behavior and the Measurement of Social Welfare," *Econometrica* 58, 5, 1007–40 (1990).

D. W. Jorgenson, L. J. Lau, and T. M. Stoker, "Welfare Comparison under Exact Aggregation," *American Economic Review* 70, 2, 268–72 (1980).

F. Jørgensen, T. A. Mathisen, and B. Larsen, "Evaluating Transport User Benefits and Social Surplus in a Transport Market — The Case of the Norwegian Ferries," *Transport Policy* 18, 1, 76–84 (2011).

L. R. Klein and H. Rubin, "A Constant-Utility Index of the Cost of Living," *Review of Economic Studies* 15, 2, 84–7 (1947).

J. Klugman, F. Rodríguez, and H.-J. Choi, "The HDI 2010: New Controversies, Old Critiques," *Journal of Economic Inequality* 9, 2, 249–88 (2011).

L. J. Lau, "Duality and the Structure of Utility Functions," *Journal of Economic Theory* 1, 374–96 (1970).

W. W. Leontief, *The Structure of American Economy, 1919–1939: An Empirical Application of Equilibrium Analysis*, Second edition enlarged, Oxford University Press, New York, (1951).

A. Lewbel, "AIDS, Translog, and the Gorman Polar Form," *Economics Letters* 24, 161–3 (1987).

A. Lewbel, "Exact Aggregation, Distribution Parameterizations, and a Nonlinear Representative Consumer," in G. F. Rhodes and T. B. Fomby (eds.): *Advances in Econometrics*, JAI Press, Greenwich, CT, 7, 253–90 (1988).

A. Lewbel, "A Path-Independent Divisia-Like Index for PIGLOG Preferences," *Economica* 56, 221, 121–3 (1989).

A. Lewbel, "Exact Aggregation and A Representative Consumer," *Quarterly Journal of Economics* 104, 3 (1989a).

A. Lewbel, "The Rank of Demand Systems: Theory and Nonparametric Estimation," *Econometrica* 59, 3, 711–30 (1991).

J. Liao and W. Wang, "Income Elasticity and International Income Differences," *Economics Letters* 169, 68–71 (2018).

A. Marshall, *Principles of Economics*, Macmillan, London, (1920).

D. McFadden, "The New Science of Pleasure: Consumer Choice Behavior and the Measurement of Well-Being," in S. Hess and A. Daly, (eds.): *Handbook of Choice Modelling* 2, Edward Elgar Publishing, Cheltenham, UK and Northampton, MA, 7–48 (2014).

D. S. Meade, "Early Days of the Input-Output Table," in T. ten Raa (ed.): *Handbook of Input-Output Analysis*, Edward Elgar

Publishing, Cheltenham, UK and Northampton, MA, 7–40 (2017).

H. Mizobuchi, "Measuring World Better Life Frontier: A Composite Indicator for OECD Better Life Index," *Social Indicators Research* 118, 3, 987–1007 (2014).

E. J. Mishan, "The Plain Truth about Consumer Surplus," *Zeitschrift für Nationalökonomie* 37, 1–2, 1–24 (1977).

H. Mohring, "Alternative Welfare Gain and Loss Measures," *Western Economic Journal* 9, 4, 349–68 (1971).

J. Muellbauer, "Aggregation, Income Distribution and Consumer Demand," *Review of Economic Studies* 42, 4, 525–43 (1975).

J. Muellbauer, "Community Preferences and the Representative Consumer," *Econometrica* 44, 5, 979–99 (1976).

S. J. Prais and H. S. Houthakker, *The Analysis of Family Budgets*, Cambridge University Press, Cambridge, (1956).

P. A. Samuelson, *Foundations of Economic Analysis*, Harvard University Press, Cambridge, MA, (1947).

P. A. Samuelson, "Some Implications of 'Linearity'," *Review of Economic Studies* 15, 2, 88–90 (1947a).

H.-A. Schwarz, "Communication," *Archives des Sciences Physiques et Naturelles* 48, 38–44 (1873).

M. D. Shapiro and D. W. Wilcox, "Measurement in the Consumer Price Index: An Evaluation," *NBER Working Paper Series* 5590 (1996).

E. Silberberg, "Duality and the Many Consumer's Surpluses," *American Economic Review* 62, 5, 942–52 (1972).

D. O. Stahl II, "Quasi-homothetic Preferences, the Generalized Divisia Quantity Index, and Aggregation," *Economica* New Series 50, 197, 87–93 (1983).

D. O. Stahl II, "A Note on the Consumer Surplus Path-of-Integration Problem," *Economica* New Series 50, 197, 95–8 (1983).

Statistics Netherlands (CBS), *Monitor of Well-being & the Sustainable Development Goals* (2020).

R. Stone, "Linear Expenditure Systems and Demand Analysis: An Application to the Pattern of British demand," *Economic Journal* 64, 255, 511–27 (1954).

A. Takayama, "On Consumer's Surplus," *Economics Letters* 10, 35–42 (1982).

T. ten Raa, "Debreu's Coefficient of Resource Utilization, the Solow Residual, and TFP: The Connection by Leontief Preferences," *Journal of Productivity Analysis* 30, 191–9 (2008).

T. ten Raa, *Microeconomics: Equilibrium & Efficiency*, Palgrave Macmillan, Basingstoke, (2013).

T. ten Raa and V. Shestalova, "Supply-Use Framework for International Environmental Policy Analysis," *Economic Systems Research* 27, 1, 77–94 (2015).

T. ten Raa, "Consumer Surplus and CES Demand," *Oxford Economic Papers* 67, 4, 1165–73 (2015a).

T. ten Raa, "Homothetic Utility, Roy's Lemma and Consumer's Surplus," *Economics Letters* 161, 133–4 (2017).

T. ten Raa, "The Consumer's Index," *International Journal of Economic Theory* 16, 119–22 (2020).

United Nations Children's Fund (UNICEF), *Multiple Indicator Cluster Surveys*, New York. http://mics.unicef.org. Accessed 15 July 2020.

United Nations Development Programme, *2020 Human Development Report*, United Nations, New York (2020).

United Nations Department of Economic and Social Affairs (UNDESA), *World Population Prospects: The 2019 Revision*, Rev. 1 (2019), New York. https://population.un.org/wpp/. Accessed 30 April 2020.

United Nations Educational, Scientific and Cultural Organization (UNESCO), Institute for Statistics, *Data Centre* (2020). http://data.uis.unesco.org. Accessed 21 July 2020.

United Nations Statistics Division, *National Accounts Main Aggregates Database* (2020). http://unstats.un.org/unsd/snaama. Accessed 15 July 2020.

R. D. Willig, "Consumer's Surplus Without Apology," *American Economic Review* 66, 4, 589–97 (1976).

World Bank, *World Development Indicators Database*, Washington, DC (2020). http://data.worldbank.org. Accessed 22 July 2020.

Index

Printed in the United States
by Baker & Taylor Publisher Services